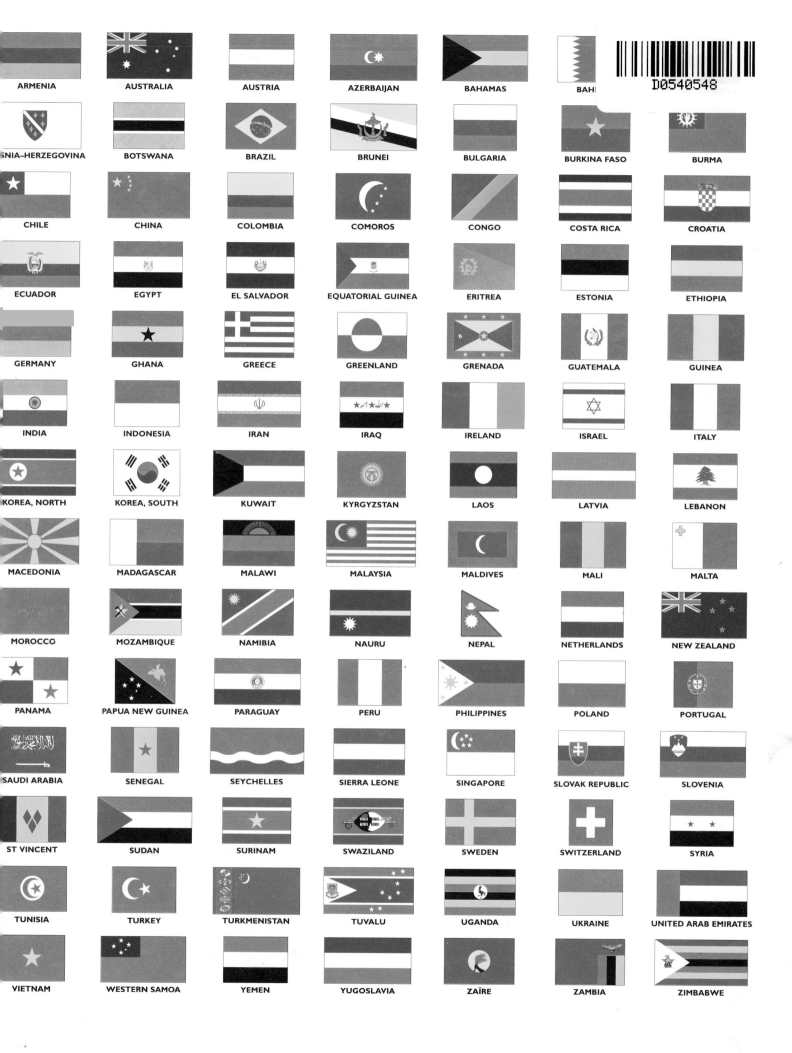

ARMENIA AUSTRALIA AUSTRIA AZERBAIJAN BAHAMAS BAH...

D0540548

...SNIA–HERZEGOVINA BOTSWANA BRAZIL BRUNEI BULGARIA BURKINA FASO BURMA

CHILE CHINA COLOMBIA COMOROS CONGO COSTA RICA CROATIA

ECUADOR EGYPT EL SALVADOR EQUATORIAL GUINEA ERITREA ESTONIA ETHIOPIA

GERMANY GHANA GREECE GREENLAND GRENADA GUATEMALA GUINEA

INDIA INDONESIA IRAN IRAQ IRELAND ISRAEL ITALY

KOREA, NORTH KOREA, SOUTH KUWAIT KYRGYZSTAN LAOS LATVIA LEBANON

MACEDONIA MADAGASCAR MALAWI MALAYSIA MALDIVES MALI MALTA

MOROCCO MOZAMBIQUE NAMIBIA NAURU NEPAL NETHERLANDS NEW ZEALAND

PANAMA PAPUA NEW GUINEA PARAGUAY PERU PHILIPPINES POLAND PORTUGAL

SAUDI ARABIA SENEGAL SEYCHELLES SIERRA LEONE SINGAPORE SLOVAK REPUBLIC SLOVENIA

ST VINCENT SUDAN SURINAM SWAZILAND SWEDEN SWITZERLAND SYRIA

TUNISIA TURKEY TURKMENISTAN TUVALU UGANDA UKRAINE UNITED ARAB EMIRATES

VIETNAM WESTERN SAMOA YEMEN YUGOSLAVIA ZAÏRE ZAMBIA ZIMBABWE

PHILIP'S

FAMILY
WORLD
ATLAS

PHILIP'S

FAMILY WORLD ATLAS

Published in Great Britain in 1996
by George Philip Limited,
an imprint of Reed Books,
Michelin House, 81 Fulham Road, London SW3 6RB,
and Auckland, Melbourne, Singapore and Toronto

Copyright © 1996 Reed International Books Limited

Cartography by Philip's

ISBN 0–540–06381–9

A CIP catalogue record for this book is available from the British Library

Printed in Hong Kong

Contents

World Statistics: Countries

This alphabetical list includes all the countries and territories of the world. If a territory is not independent, then the country it is associated with is named. The area figures give the total area of land, inland water and ice.

The units for areas and populations are thousands. The population figures are 1995 estimates. The annual income is the Gross National Product per capita in US dollars. The figures are the latest available, usually 1993–4.

COUNTRY/TERRITORY	AREA km² 1,000s	AREA miles² 1,000s	POPULATION 1,000s	CAPITAL	ANNUAL INCOME US $
Afghanistan	652	252	19,509	Kabul	220
Albania	28.8	11.1	3,458	Tirana	340
Algeria	2,382	920	25,012	Algiers	1,650
American Samoa (US)	0.20	0.08	58	Pago Pago	2,600
Andorra	0.45	0.17	65	Andorra La Vella	14,000
Angola	1,247	481	10,020	Luanda	600
Anguilla (UK)	0.1	0.04	8	The Valley	6,800
Antigua & Barbuda	0.44	0.17	67	St John's	6,390
Argentina	2,767	1,068	34,663	Buenos Aires	7,290
Armenia	29.8	11.5	3,603	Yerevan	660
Aruba (Neths)	0.19	0.07	71	Oranjestad	17,500
Ascension Is. (UK)	0.09	0.03	1.5	Georgetown	–
Australia	7,687	2,968	18,107	Canberra	17,510
Australian Antarctic Territory (Australia)	6,120	2,363	0	–	–
Austria	83.9	32.4	8,004	Vienna	23,120
Azerbaijan	86.6	33.4	7,559	Baku	730
Azores (Port.)	2.2	0.87	238	Ponta Delgada	–
Bahamas	13.9	5.4	277	Nassau	11,500
Bahrain	0.68	0.26	558	Manama	7,870
Bangladesh	144	56	118,342	Dhaka	220
Barbados	0.43	0.17	263	Bridgetown	6,240
Belarus	207.6	80.1	10,500	Minsk	2,930
Belgium	30.5	11.8	10,140	Brussels	21,210
Belize	23	8.9	216	Belmopan	2,440
Benin	113	43	5,381	Porto-Novo	420
Bermuda (UK)	0.05	0.02	64	Hamilton	27,000
Bhutan	47	18.1	1,639	Thimphu	170
Bolivia	1,099	424	7,900	La Paz/Sucre	770
Bosnia-Herzegovina	51	20	3,800	Sarajevo	2,500
Botswana	582	225	1,481	Gaborone	2,590
Bouvet Is. (Nor.)	0.05	0.02	0.02	–	–
Brazil	8,512	3,286	161,416	Brasília	3,020
British Antarctic Terr. (UK)	1,709	660	0.3	–	–
Brunei	5.8	2.2	284	Bandar Seri Begawan	9,000
Bulgaria	111	43	8,771	Sofia	1,160
Burkina Faso	274	106	10,326	Ouagadougou	300
Burma (= Myanmar)	677	261	46,580	Rangoon	950
Burundi	27.8	10.7	6,412	Bujumbura	180
Cambodia	181	70	10,452	Phnom Penh	600
Cameroon	475	184	13,232	Yaoundé	770
Canada	9,976	3,852	29,972	Ottawa	20,670
Canary Is. (Spain)	7.3	2.8	1,494	Las Palmas/Santa Cruz	–
Cape Verde Is.	4	1.6	386	Praia	870
Cayman Is. (UK)	0.26	0.10	31	George Town	20,000
Central African Republic	623	241	3,294	Bangui	390
Chad	1,284	496	6,314	Ndjaména	200
Chatham Is. (NZ)	0.96	0.37	0.05	Waitangi	–
Chile	757	292	14,271	Santiago	3,070
China	9,597	3,705	1,226,944	Beijing	490
Christmas Is. (Aus.)	0.14	0.05	2	The Settlement	–
Cocos (Keeling) Is. (Aus.)	0.01	0.005	0.6	West Island	–
Colombia	1,139	440	34,948	Bogotá	1,400
Comoros	2.2	0.86	654	Moroni	520
Congo	342	132	2,593	Brazzaville	920
Cook Is. (NZ)	0.24	0.09	19	Avarua	900
Costa Rica	51.1	19.7	3,436	San José	2,160
Croatia	56.5	21.8	4,900	Zagreb	4,500
Crozet Is. (Fr.)	0.51	0.19	35	–	–
Cuba	111	43	11,050	Havana	1,250
Cyprus	9.3	3.6	742	Nicosia	10,380
Czech Republic	78.9	30.4	10,500	Prague	2,730
Denmark	43.1	16.6	5,229	Copenhagen	26,510
Djibouti	23.2	9	603	Djibouti	780
Dominica	0.75	0.29	89	Roseau	2,680

COUNTRY/TERRITORY	AREA km² 1,000s	AREA miles² 1,000s	POPULATION 1,000s	CAPITAL	ANNUAL INCOME US $
Dominican Republic	48.7	18.8	7,818	Santo Domingo	1,080
Ecuador	284	109	11,384	Quito	1,170
Egypt	1,001	387	64,100	Cairo	660
El Salvador	21	8.1	5,743	San Salvador	1,320
Equatorial Guinea	28.1	10.8	400	Malabo	360
Eritrea	94	36	3,850	Asmara	500
Estonia	44.7	17.3	1,531	Tallinn	3,040
Ethiopia	1,128	436	51,600	Addis Ababa	100
Falkland Is. (UK)	12.2	4.7	2	Stanley	–
Faroe Is. (Den.)	1.4	0.54	47	Tórshavn	23,660
Fiji	18.3	7.1	773	Suva	2,140
Finland	338	131	5,125	Helsinki	18,970
France	552	213	58,286	Paris	22,360
French Guiana (Fr.)	90	34.7	154	Cayenne	5,000
French Polynesia (Fr.)	4	1.5	217	Papeete	7,000
Gabon	268	103	1,316	Libreville	4,050
Gambia, The	11.3	4.4	1,144	Banjul	360
Georgia	69.7	26.9	5,448	Tbilisi	560
Germany	357	138	82,000	Berlin/Bonn	23,560
Ghana	239	92	17,462	Accra	430
Gibraltar (UK)	0.007	0.003	28	Gibraltar Town	5,000
Greece	132	51	10,510	Athens	7,390
Greenland (Den.)	2,176	840	59	Godthåb (= Nuuk)	9,000
Grenada	0.34	0.13	94	St George's	2,410
Guadeloupe (Fr.)	1.7	0.66	443	Basse-Terre	9,000
Guam (US)	0.55	0.21	155	Agana	6,000
Guatemala	109	42	10,624	Guatemala City	1,110
Guinea	246	95	6,702	Conakry	510
Guinea-Bissau	36.1	13.9	1,073	Bissau	220
Guyana	215	83	832	Georgetown	350
Haiti	27.8	10.7	7,180	Port-au-Prince	800
Honduras	112	43	5,940	Tegucigalpa	580
Hong Kong (UK)	1.1	0.40	6,000	–	17,860
Hungary	93	35.9	10,500	Budapest	3,330
Iceland	103	40	269	Reykjavik	23,620
India	3,288	1,269	942,989	New Delhi	290
Indonesia	1,905	735	198,644	Jakarta	730
Iran	1,648	636	68,885	Tehran	4,750
Iraq	438	169	20,184	Baghdad	2,000
Ireland	70.3	27.1	3,589	Dublin	12,580
Israel	27	10.3	5,696	Jerusalem	13,760
Italy	301	116	57,181	Rome	19,620
Ivory Coast	322	125	14,271	Yamoussoukro	630
Jamaica	11	4.2	2,700	Kingston	1,390
Japan	378	146	125,156	Tokyo	31,450
Johnston Is. (US)	0.002	0.0009	1	–	–
Jordan	89.2	34.4	5,547	Amman	1,190
Kazakstan	2,717	1,049	17,099	Alma-Ata	1,540
Kenya	580	224	28,240	Nairobi	270
Kerguelen Is. (Fr.)	7.2	2.8	0.7	–	–
Kermadec Is. (NZ)	0.03	0.01	0.1	–	–
Kiribati	0.72	0.28	80	Tarawa	710
Korea, North	121	47	23,931	Pyongyang	1,100
Korea, South	99	38.2	45,088	Seoul	7,670
Kuwait	17.8	6.9	1,668	Kuwait City	23,350
Kyrgyzstan	198.5	76.6	4,738	Bishkek	830

COUNTRY/TERRITORY	AREA km² 1,000s	AREA miles² 1,000s	POPULATION 1,000s	CAPITAL	ANNUAL INCOME US $
Laos	237	91	4,906	Vientiane	290
Latvia	65	25	2,558	Riga	2,030
Lebanon	10.4	4	2,971	Beirut	1,750
Lesotho	30.4	11.7	2,064	Maseru	660
Liberia	111	43	3,092	Monrovia	800
Libya	1,760	679	5,410	Tripoli	6,500
Liechtenstein	0.16	0.06	31	Vaduz	33,510
Lithuania	65.2	25.2	3,735	Vilnius	1,310
Luxembourg	2.6	1	408	Luxembourg	35,850
Macau (Port.)	0.02	0.006	490	Macau	7,500
Macedonia	25.3	9.8	2,173	Skopje	730
Madagascar	587	227	15,206	Antananarivo	240
Madeira (Port.)	0.81	0.31	253	Funchal	–
Malawi	118	46	9,800	Lilongwe	220
Malaysia	330	127	20,174	Kuala Lumpur	3,160
Maldives	0.30	0.12	254	Malé	820
Mali	1,240	479	10,700	Bamako	300
Malta	0.32	0.12	367	Valletta	6,800
Marshall Is.	0.18	0.07	55	Dalap-Uliga-Darrit	1,500
Martinique (Fr.)	1.1	0.42	384	Fort-de-France	3,500
Mauritania	1,025	396	2,268	Nouakchott	510
Mauritius	2.0	0.72	1,112	Port Louis	2,980
Mayotte (Fr.)	0.37	0.14	101	Mamoundzou	1,430
Mexico	1,958	756	93,342	Mexico City	3,750
Micronesia, Federated States of	0.70	0.27	125	Palikir	1,560
Midway Is. (US)	0.005	0.002	2	–	–
Moldova	33.7	13	4,434	Kishinev	1,180
Monaco	0.002	0.0001	32	Monaco	16,000
Mongolia	1,567	605	2,408	Ulan Bator	400
Montserrat (UK)	0.10	0.04	11	Plymouth	4,500
Morocco	447	172	26,857	Rabat	1,030
Mozambique	802	309	17,800	Maputo	80
Namibia	825	318	1,610	Windhoek	1,660
Nauru	0.02	0.008	12	Yaren District	10,000
Nepal	141	54	21,953	Katmandu	160
Netherlands	41.5	16	15,495	Amsterdam/The Hague	20,710
Neths Antilles (Neths)	0.99	0.38	199	Willemstad	9,700
New Caledonia (Fr.)	19	7.3	181	Nouméa	6,000
New Zealand	269	104	3,567	Wellington	12,900
Nicaragua	130	50	4,544	Managua	360
Niger	1,267	489	9,149	Niamey	270
Nigeria	924	357	88,515	Abuja	310
Niue (NZ)	0.26	0.10	2	Alofi	–
Norfolk Is. (Aus.)	0.03	0.01	2	Kingston	–
Northern Mariana Is. (US)	0.48	0.18	47	Saipan	11,500
Norway	324	125	4,361	Oslo	26,340
Oman	212	82	2,252	Muscat	5,600
Pakistan	796	307	143,595	Islamabad	430
Palau	0.46	0.18	17	Koror	2,260
Panama	77.1	29.8	2,629	Panama City	2,580
Papua New Guinea	463	179	4,292	Port Moresby	1,120
Paraguay	407	157	4,979	Asunción	1,500
Peru	1,285	496	23,588	Lima	1,490
Philippines	300	116	67,167	Manila	830
Pitcairn Is. (UK)	0.03	0.01	0.06	Adamstown	–
Poland	313	121	38,587	Warsaw	2,270
Portugal	92.4	35.7	10,600	Lisbon	7,890
Puerto Rico (US)	9	3.5	3,689	San Juan	7,020
Qatar	11	4.2	594	Doha	15,140
Réunion (Fr.)	2.5	0.97	655	Saint-Denis	3,900
Romania	238	92	22,863	Bucharest	1,120
Ross Dependency (NZ)	435	168	0	–	–
Russia	17,075	6,592	148,385	Moscow	2,350
Rwanda	26.3	10.2	7,899	Kigali	200

COUNTRY/TERRITORY	AREA km² 1,000s	AREA miles² 1,000s	POPULATION 1,000s	CAPITAL	ANNUAL INCOME US $
St Helena (UK)	0.12	0.05	6	Jamestown	–
St Kitts & Nevis	0.36	0.14	45	Basseterre	4,470
St Lucia	0.62	0.24	147	Castries	3,040
St Pierre & Miquelon (Fr.)	0.24	0.09	6	Saint Pierre	–
St Vincent & the Grenadines	0.39	0.15	111	Kingstown	1,730
San Marino	0.06	0.02	26	San Marino	20,000
São Tomé & Príncipe	0.96	0.37	133	São Tomé	330
Saudi Arabia	2,150	830	18,395	Riyadh	8,000
Senegal	197	76	8,308	Dakar	730
Seychelles	0.46	0.18	75	Victoria	6,370
Sierra Leone	71.7	27.7	4,467	Freetown	140
Singapore	0.62	0.24	2,990	Singapore	19,310
Slovak Republic	49	18.9	5,400	Bratislava	1,900
Slovenia	20.3	7.8	2,000	Ljubljana	6,310
Solomon Is.	28.9	11.2	378	Honiara	750
Somalia	638	246	9,180	Mogadishu	500
South Africa	1,220	471	44,000	Cape Town/Pretoria /Bloemfontein	2,900
South Georgia (UK)	3.8	1.4	0.05	–	–
Spain	505	195	39,664	Madrid	13,650
Sri Lanka	65.6	25.3	18,359	Colombo	600
Sudan	2,506	967	29,980	Khartoum	750
Surinam	163	63	421	Paramaribo	1,210
Svalbard (Nor.)	62.9	24.3	4	Longyearbyen	–
Swaziland	17.4	6.7	849	Mbabane	1,050
Sweden	450	174	8,893	Stockholm	24,830
Switzerland	41.3	15.9	7,268	Bern	36,410
Syria	185	71	14,614	Damascus	5,700
Taiwan	36	13.9	21,100	Taipei	11,000
Tajikistan	143.1	55.2	6,102	Dushanbe	470
Tanzania	945	365	29,710	Dodoma	100
Thailand	513	198	58,432	Bangkok	2,040
Togo	56.8	21.9	4,140	Lomé	330
Tokelau (NZ)	0.01	0.005	2	Nukunonu	–
Tonga	0.75	0.29	107	Nuku'alofa	1,610
Trinidad & Tobago	5.1	2	1,295	Port of Spain	3,730
Tristan da Cunha (UK)	0.11	0.04	0.33	Edinburgh	–
Tunisia	164	63	8,906	Tunis	1,780
Turkey	779	301	61,303	Ankara	2,120
Turkmenistan	488.1	188.5	4,100	Ashkhabad	1,400
Turks & Caicos Is. (UK)	0.43	0.17	15	Cockburn Town	5,000
Tuvalu	0.03	0.01	10	Fongafale	600
Uganda	236	91	21,466	Kampala	190
Ukraine	603.7	233.1	52,027	Kiev	1,910
United Arab Emirates	83.6	32.3	2,800	Abu Dhabi	22,470
United Kingdom	243.3	94	58,306	London	17,970
United States of America	9,373	3,619	263,563	Washington, DC	24,750
Uruguay	177	68	3,186	Montevideo	3,910
Uzbekistan	447.4	172.7	22,833	Tashkent	960
Vanuatu	12.2	4.7	167	Port-Vila	1,230
Vatican City	0.0004	0.0002	1	–	–
Venezuela	912	352	21,800	Caracas	2,840
Vietnam	332	127	74,580	Hanoi	170
Virgin Is. (UK)	0.15	0.06	20	Road Town	–
Virgin Is. (US)	0.34	0.13	105	Charlotte Amalie	12,000
Wake Is.	0.008	0.003	0.30	–	–
Wallis & Futuna Is. (Fr.)	0.20	0.08	13	Mata-Utu	–
Western Sahara	266	103	220	El Aaiún	300
Western Samoa	2.8	1.1	169	Apia	980
Yemen	528	204	14,609	Sana	800
Yugoslavia	102.3	39.5	10,881	Belgrade	1,000
Zaïre	2,345	905	44,504	Kinshasa	500
Zambia	753	291	9,500	Lusaka	370
Zimbabwe	391	151	11,453	Harare	540

World Statistics: Cities

This list shows the principal cities with more than 500,000 inhabitants (for Brazil, China, India, Iran and Japan only cities with more than 1 million inhabitants are included). The figures are taken from the most recent census or estimate, and are the population of the metropolitan area, e.g. greater New York, Mexico or London. All the figures are in thousands. Local name forms have been used for the smaller cities (e.g. Kraków).

Afghanistan
Kabul 1,424

Algeria
Algiers 1,722
Oran 664

Angola
Luanda 1,544

Argentina
Buenos Aires 11,256
Córdoba 1,198
Rosario 1,096
Mendoza 775
La Plata 640
San Miguel de Tucumán 622
Mar del Plata 520

Armenia
Yerevan 1,254

Australia
Sydney 3,657
Melbourne 3,081
Perth 1,193
Adelaide 1,050
Brisbane 777

Austria
Vienna 1,560

Azerbaijan
Baku 1,149

Bangladesh
Dhaka 6,105
Chittagong 2,041
Khulna 877
Rajshahi 517

Belarus
Minsk 1,613
Gomel 506

Belgium
Brussels 952

Bolivia
La Paz 1,126
Santa Cruz 695

Bosnia-Herzegovina
Sarajevo 526

Brazil
São Paulo 9,480
Rio de Janeiro 5,336
Salvador 2,056
Belo Horizonte 2,049
Fortaleza 1,758
Brasília 1,596
Curitiba 1,290
Recife 1,290
Nova Iguaçu 1,286
Pôrto Alegre 1,263
Belém 1,246
Manaus 1,011

Bulgaria
Sofia 1,221

Burkina Faso
Ouagadougou 634

Burma (Myanmar)
Rangoon 2,513
Mandalay 533

Cambodia
Phnom Penh 900

Cameroon
Douala 884
Yaoundé 750

Canada
Toronto 3,893
Montréal 3,127
Vancouver 1,603
Ottawa-Hull 921
Edmonton 840
Calgary 754
Winnipeg 652
Québec 646
Hamilton 600

Central African Rep.
Bangui 597

Chad
Ndjaména 530

Chile
Santiago 5,343

China
Shanghai 8,930
Beijing 6,690
Tianjin 5,000
Shenyang 4,050
Chongqing 3,870
Wuhan 3,870
Guangzhou 3,750
Harbin 3,120
Chengdu 2,760
Nanjing 2,490
Changchun 2,470
Xi'an 2,410
Dalian 2,400
Zibo 2,400
Qingdao 2,300
Jinan 2,150
Hangzhou 1,790
Taiyuan 1,720
Zhengzhou 1,690
Shijiazhuang 1,610
Changsha 1,510
Kunming 1,500
Nanchang 1,440
Fuzhou 1,380
Lanzhou 1,340
Anshan 1,204
Fushun 1,202
Ürümqi 1,130
Hefei 1,110
Ningbo 1,100
Guiyang 1,080
Qiqihar 1,070
Tangshan 1,044
Jilin 1,037
Linhai 1,012
Macheng 1,010

Colombia
Bogotá 5,132
Cali 1,687
Medellin 1,608
Barranquilla 1,049
Cartagena 726

Congo
Brazzaville 938
Pointe-Noire 576

Croatia
Zagreb 931

Cuba
Havana 2,119

Czech Republic
Prague 1,216

Denmark
Copenhagen 1,337

Dominican Republic
Santo Domingo 2,200

Ecuador
Guayaquil 1,508
Quito 1,101

Egypt
Cairo 6,800
Alexandria 3,380
El Gîza 2,144
Shubra el K. 834

El Salvador
San Salvador 1,522

Ethiopia
Addis Ababa 2,213

Finland
Helsinki 516

France
Paris 9,319
Lyons 1,262
Marseilles 1,087
Lille 959
Bordeaux 696
Toulouse 650
Nice 516

Georgia
Tbilisi 1,279

Germany
Berlin 3,475
Hamburg 1,703
Munich 1,256
Cologne 693
Frankfurt 660
Essen 622
Dortmund 602
Stuttgart 594
Düsseldorf 575
Bremen 552
Duisburg 537
Hannover 525

Ghana
Accra 965

Greece
Athens 3,097

Guatemala
Guatemala 2,000

Guinea
Conakry 810

Haiti
Port-au-Prince 1,402

Honduras
Tegucigalpa 679

Hong Kong
Kowloon 2,031
Hong Kong 1,251
Tsuen Wan 690

Hungary
Budapest 2,009

India
Bombay 12,572
Calcutta 10,916
Delhi 7,207
Madras 5,361
Hyderabad 4,280
Bangalore 4,087
Ahmadabad 3,298
Pune 2,485
Kanpur 2,111
Nagpur 1,661
Lucknow 1,642
Surat 1,517
Jaipur 1,514
Coimbatore 1,136
Vadodara 1,115
Indore 1,104
Patna 1,099
Madurai 1,094
Bhopal 1,064
Vishakha-patnam 1,052
Varanasi 1,026
Ludhiana 1,012

Indonesia
Jakarta 8,259
Surabaya 2,421
Medan 1,686
Bandung 2,027
Palembang 1,084
Semarang 1,005
Ujung Pandang 913
Malang 650
Surakarta 504

Iran
Tehran 6,476
Mashhad 1,759
Esfahan 1,127
Tabriz 1,089

Iraq
Baghdad 3,841
Diyala 961
As Sulaymaniyah 952
Arbil 770
Al Mawsil 644
Kadhimain 521

Ireland
Dublin 1,024

Israel
Jerusalem 544

Italy
Rome 2,723
Milan 1,359
Naples 1,072
Turin 953
Palermo 697
Genoa 668

Ivory Coast
Abidjan 1,929

Jamaica
Kingston 644

Japan
Tokyo 11,927
Yokohama 3,288
Osaka 2,589
Nagoya 2,159
Sapporo 1,732
Kobe 1,509
Kyoto 1,452
Fukuoka 1,269
Kawasaki 1,200
Hiroshima 1,102
Kitakyushu 1,020

Jordan
Amman 1,272
Az-Zarqā 605

Kazakstan
Alma-Ata 1,147
Karaganda 613

Kenya
Nairobi 1,429

Korea, North
Pyŏngyang 2,639
Hamhung 775
Chŏngjin 754
Chinnampo 691
Sinŭiju 500

Korea, South
Seoul 10,628
Pusan 3,798
Taegu 2,229
Inchon 1,818
Kwangju 1,145
Taejŏn 1,062
Ulsan 683
Puch'on 668
Suwŏn 645
Sŏngnam 541
Chŏnju 517

Kyrgyzstan
Bishkek 628

Latvia
Riga 840

Lebanon
Beirut 1,500
Tripoli 500

Libya
Tripoli 990

Lithuania
Vilnius 576

Macedonia
Skopje 563

Madagascar
Antananarivo 1,053

Malaysia
Kuala Lumpur 1,145

Mali
Bamako 746

Mauritania
Nouakchott 600

Mexico
Mexico City 15,048
Guadalajara 2,847
Monterrey 2,522
Puebla 1,055
León 872
Ciudad Juárez 798
Tijuana 743
Culiacán Rosales 602
Mexicali 602
Acapulco de Juárez 592
Mérida 557
Chihuahua 530
San Luis Potosí 526
Aguascalientés 506

Moldova
Kishinev 667

Mongolia
Ulan Bator 601

Morocco
Casablanca 3,079
Rabat-Salé 1,344
Fès 735
Marrakesh 665
Oujda 661

Mozambique
Maputo 1,070

Netherlands
Amsterdam 1,091
Rotterdam 1,069
The Hague 694
Utrecht 543

New Zealand
Auckland 896

Nicaragua
Managua 974

Nigeria
Lagos 1,347
Ibadan 1,295
Kano 700
Ogbomosho 661

Norway
Oslo 714

Pakistan
Karachi 5,181
Lahore 2,953
Faisalabad 1,104
Rawalpindi 795
Hyderabad 752
Multan 722
Gujranwala 659
Peshawar 556

Panama
Panama City 584

Paraguay
Asunción 945

Peru
Lima-Callao 6,601
Callao 638
Arequipa 620

Philippines
Manila 6,720
Quezon City 1,667
Davao 868
Cebu 641
Caloocan 629

Poland
Warsaw 1,655
Lódz 847
Kraków 751
Wroclaw 643
Poznań 590

Portugal
Lisbon 2,561
Porto 1,174

Puerto Rico
San Juan 1,816

Romania
Bucharest 2,067

Russia
Moscow 8,957
St Petersburg 5,004
Novosibirsk 1,472
Nizhniy Novgorod 1,451
Yekaterinburg 1,413
Samara 1,271
Omsk 1,193
Chelyabinsk 1,170
Perm 1,108
Kazan 1,107
Ufa 1,100
Volgograd 1,031
Rostov 1,027
Voronezh 958
Krasnoyarsk 925
Saratov 916
Krasnodar 751
Togliatti 677
Vladivostok 675
Barnaul 665
Izhevsk 651
Irkutsk 644
Simbirsk 638
Yaroslavl 637
Khabarovsk 626
Novokuznetsk 614
Tula 591
Orenburg 574
Kemerovo 559
Penza 553
Tyumen 550
Ryazan 533
Naberezhnyye-Chelny 517
Astrakhan 512
Tomsk 506
Lipetsk 504

Saudi Arabia
Riyadh 2,000
Jedda 1,400
Mecca 618
Medina 500

Senegal
Dakar 1,730

Sierra Leone
Freetown 505

Singapore
Singapore 2,874

Somalia
Mogadishu 1,000

South Africa
Cape Town 1,912
Johannesburg 1,196
East Rand 1,379
Durban 1,137
Pretoria 1,080
Port Elizabeth 853
West Rand 870
Vanderbijlpark-Vereeniging 774
Soweto 597
Sasolburg 540

Spain
Madrid 3,041
Barcelona 1,631
Valencia 764
Seville 714
Zaragoza 607
Málaga 531

Sri Lanka
Colombo 1,863

Sudan
Khartoum 561
Omdurman 526

Sweden
Stockholm 1,539
Gothenburg 783

Switzerland
Zürich 840

Syria
Damascus 1,451
Aleppo 1,445
Homs 518

Taiwan
Taipei 2,653
Kaohsiung 1,405
Taichung 817
Tainan 700
Panchiao 544

Tajikistan
Dushanbe 602

Tanzania
Dar-es-Salaam 1,361

Thailand
Bangkok 5,876

Togo
Lomé 590

Tunisia
Tunis 1,395

Turkey
Istanbul 6,620
Ankara 2,559
Izmir 1,757
Adana 916
Bursa 835
Gaziantep 603
Konya 513

Uganda
Kampala 773

Ukraine
Kiev 2,643
Kharkov 1,622
Dnepropetr'sk 1,190
Donetsk 1,121
Odessa 1,096
Zaporozhye 898
Lvov 807
Krivoy Rog 729
Mariupol 523
Nikolayev 515
Lugansk 505

United Kingdom
London 6,967
Birmingham 1,220
Manchester 981
Glasgow 720
Liverpool 664
Leeds 529
Newcastle 525

United States
New York 19,670
Los Angeles 15,048
Chicago 8,410
San Francisco 6,410
Philadelphia 5,939
Boston 5,439
Detroit 5,246
Washington 4,360
Dallas 4,215
Houston 3,962
Miami 3,309
Atlanta 3,153
Seattle 3,131
Cleveland 2,890
Minneapolis-St Paul 2,618
San Diego 2,601
St Louis 2,519
Baltimore 2,434
Pittsburgh 2,406
Phoenix 2,330
Tampa 2,107
Denver 2,089
Portland 1,897
Cincinnati 1,865
Milwaukee 1,629
Kansas City 1,617
Sacramento 1,563
Norfolk 1,497
Indianapolis 1,424
Columbus 1,394
San Antonio 1,379
New Orleans 1,303
Charlotte 1,212
Buffalo 1,194
Hartford 1,156
Salt Lake City 1,128
Oklahoma 984
San Jose 801
Jacksonville 661
Omaha 656
Memphis 610
El Paso 544

Uruguay
Montevideo 1,384

Uzbekistan
Tashkent 2,094

Venezuela
Caracas 2,784
Maracaibo 1,364
Valencia 1,032
Maracay 800
Barquisimeto 745
Ciudad Guayana 524

Vietnam
Ho Chi Minh 3,924
Hanoi 3,056
Haiphong 1,448

Yugoslavia
Belgrade 1,137

Zaire
Kinshasa 3,804
Lubumbashi 739
Mbuji-Mayi 613
Kolwezi 544

Zambia
Lusaka 982

Zimbabwe
Harare 1,189
Bulawayo 622

GENERAL REFERENCE

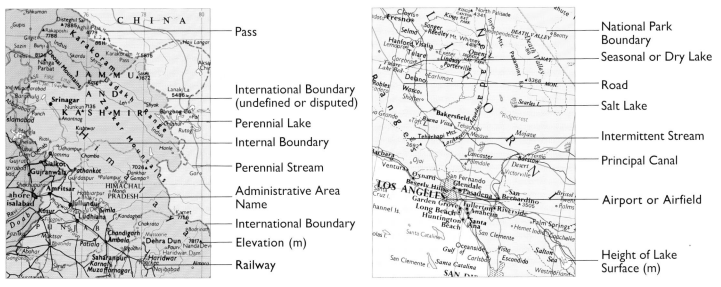

— Pass

— International Boundary (undefined or disputed)

— Perennial Lake

— Internal Boundary

— Perennial Stream

— Administrative Area Name

— International Boundary

— Elevation (m)

— Railway

— National Park Boundary

— Seasonal or Dry Lake

— Road

— Salt Lake

— Intermittent Stream

— Principal Canal

— Airport or Airfield

— Height of Lake Surface (m)

Settlements

Settlement symbols and type styles vary according to the scale of each map and indicate the importance of towns rather than specific population figures.

TIME ZONES

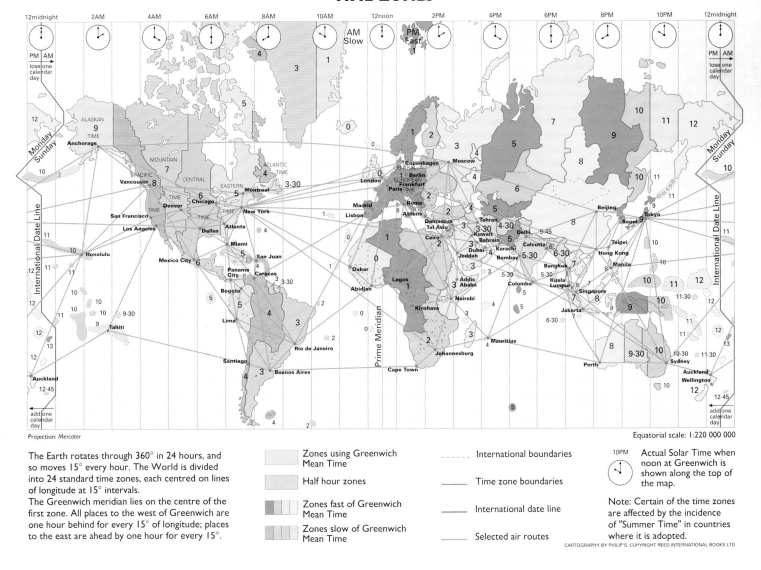

Projection: *Mercator*

Equatorial scale: 1:220 000 000

The Earth rotates through 360° in 24 hours, and so moves 15° every hour. The World is divided into 24 standard time zones, each centred on lines of longitude at 15° intervals.
The Greenwich meridian lies on the centre of the first zone. All places to the west of Greenwich are one hour behind for every 15° of longitude; places to the east are ahead by one hour for every 15°.

Zones using Greenwich Mean Time

Half hour zones

Zones fast of Greenwich Mean Time

Zones slow of Greenwich Mean Time

----- International boundaries

——— Time zone boundaries

——— International date line

——— Selected air routes

10PM Actual Solar Time when noon at Greenwich is shown along the top of the map.

Note: Certain of the time zones are affected by the incidence of "Summer Time" in countries where it is adopted.

CARTOGRAPHY BY PHILIP'S. COPYRIGHT REED INTERNATIONAL BOOKS LTD

Projection: Hammer Equal Area

Hanoi ● Capital Cities

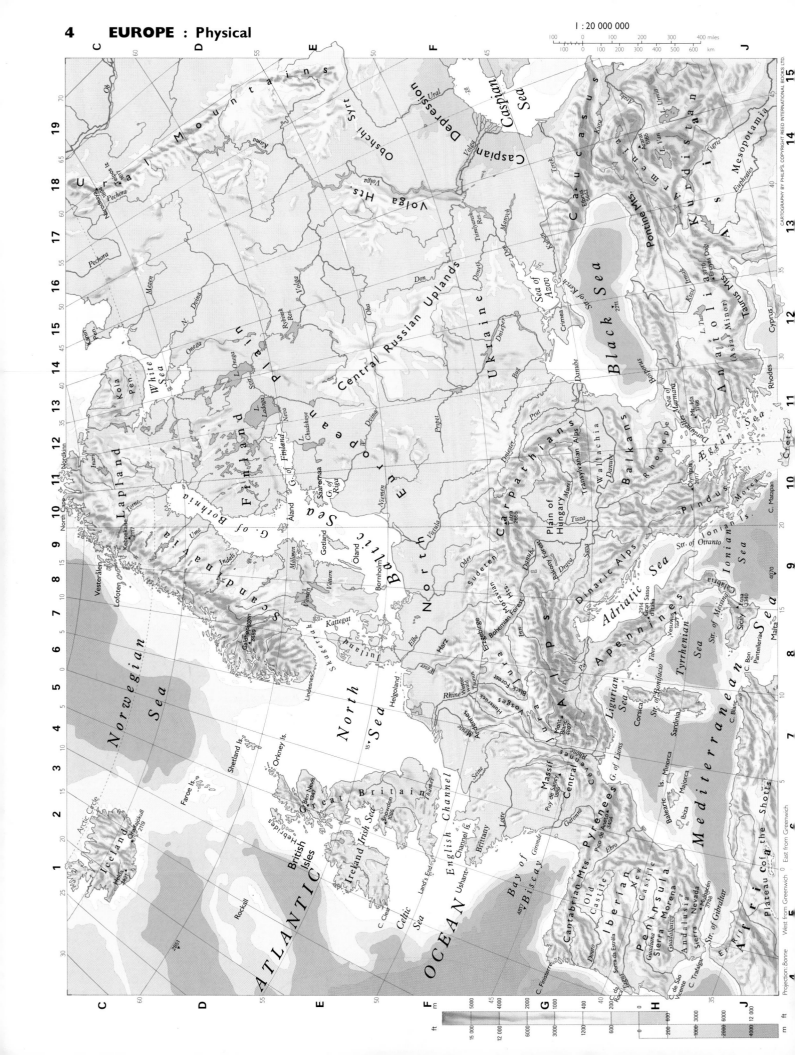

1 : 20 000 000

Projection: Bonne

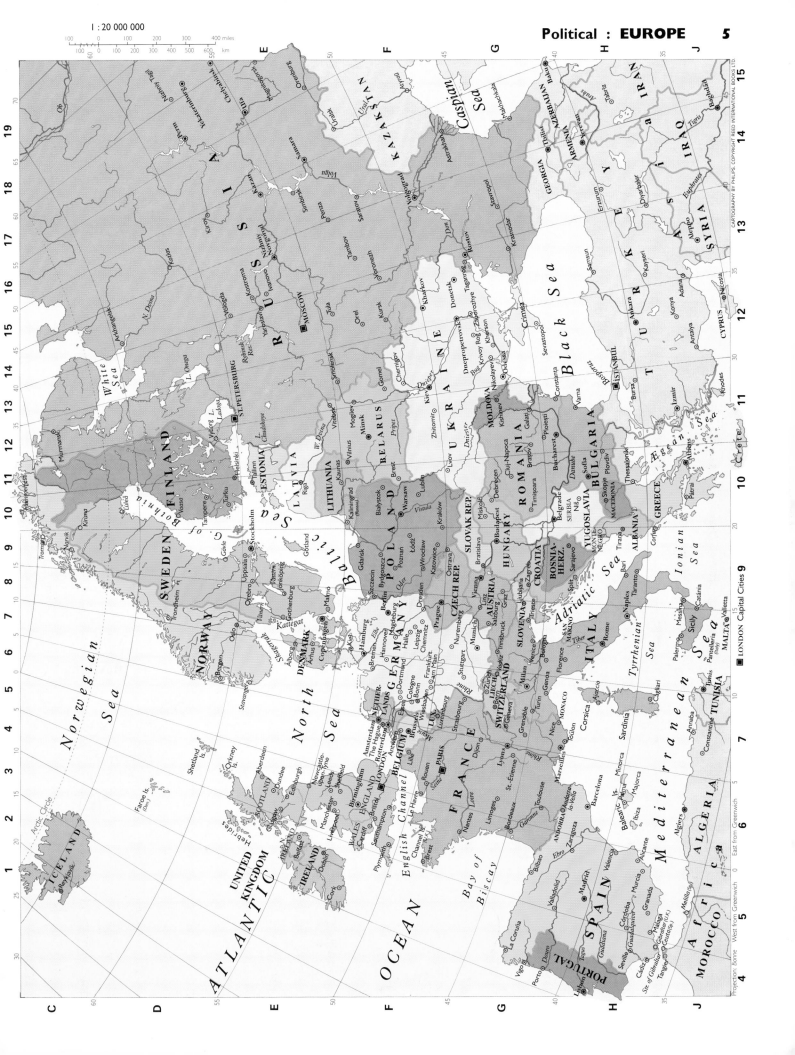

1 : 10 000 000

ICELAND
On the same scale   West from Greenwich

ATLANTIC OCEAN

ARCTIC OCEAN

Arctic Circle

N O R W A Y

S W E D E N

Norrland

Svealand

Götaland

Lapland

Kola Peninsula

White Sea

Karelia

FINLAND

Gulf of Bothnia

BALTIC SEA

Gulf of Finland

ESTONIA

LATVIA

LITHUANIA

(RUSSIA)

RUSSIA

Skagerrak

Kattegat

DENMARK

Jutland

GERMANY

POLAND

BELARUS

UKRAINE

CZECH REP.

Projection: Conical with two standard parallels

East from Greenwich

COPYRIGHT. GEORGE PHILIP & SON. LTD.

1 : 5 000 000

50 0 50 100 miles
50 0 50 100 150 km

Corsica — C. Corse / Bastia, Calvi, Corte, Mte. Rotondo 2710, Mte. Cinto, Ajaccio, Bonifacio, Porto-Vecchio 2136, 2625

Countries / regions: UNITED KINGDOM, BELGIUM, LUXEMBOURG, GERMANY, SWITZERLAND, AUSTRIA, LIECHTENSTEIN, ITALY, FRANCE, SPAIN, ANDORRA

Seas: English Channel, Bay of Biscay, MEDITERRANEAN SEA, Golfe du Lion, Golfe de Gascogne

Projection: Conical with two standard parallels

East from Greenwich / West from Greenwich

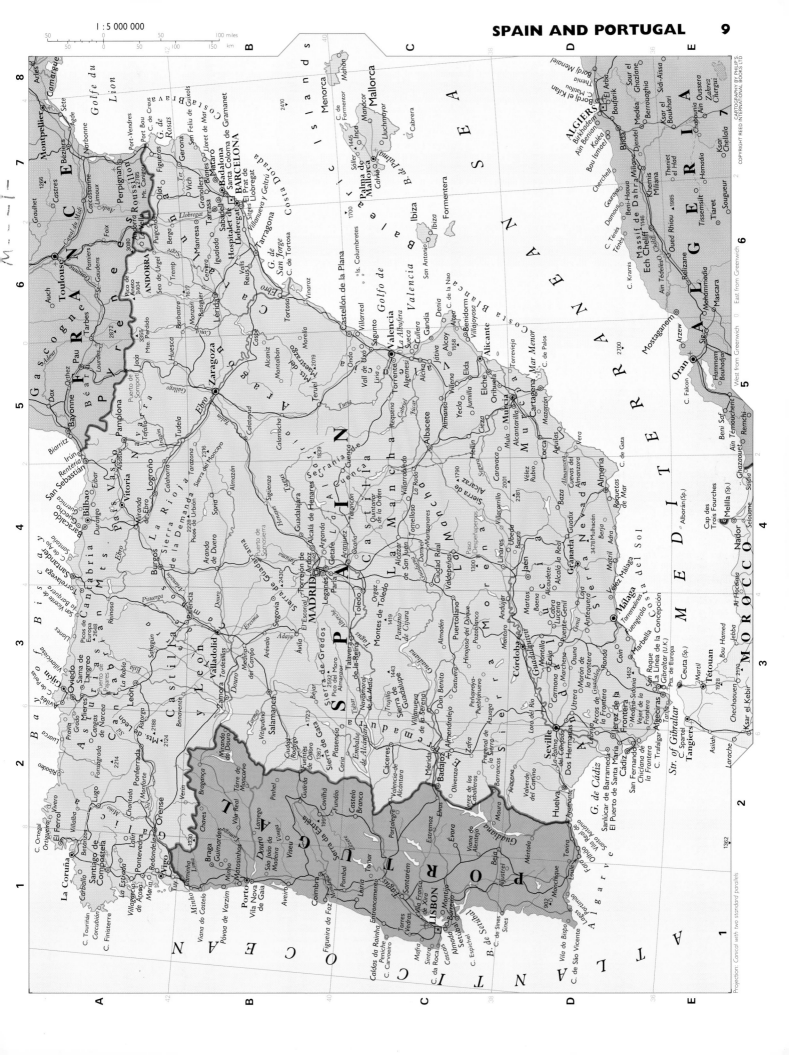

1 : 5 000 000

1 : 5 000 000

Scale markings: 50 0 50 100 miles / km 50 0 50 100 150

Grid columns (top): 9 10 11 12 13 16
Grid rows (right): B C D E F G

LITHUANIA

BELARUS

MINSK

POLAND

WARSAW

UKRAINE

KIEV

Kiev Res.

KIEV

Pripet Marsh

SLOVAK REP.

Bratislava

HUNGARY

BUDAPEST

MOLDOVA

Kishinev

Tiraspol

ROMANIA

BUCHAREST

Transylvania

Transylvanian Alps

CROATIA

BOSNIA-HERZEGOVINA

Sarajevo

YUGOSLAVIA

BELGRADE

BULGARIA

Major cities and places (selected):
Kaliningrad (Russia), Gusev, Vilnius, Marijampolė, Gdynia, Gdańsk, Elbląg, Olsztyn, Białystok, Grodno, Lida, Baranovichi, Bobruysk, Gomel, Toruń, Bydgoszcz, Płock, Łódź, Lublin, Brest, Pinsk, Mazyr, Wrocław, Kielce, Radom, Kraków, Lvov, Lutsk, Rovno, Zhitomir, Katowice, Košice, Uzhhorod, Ivano-Frankovsk, Chernovtsy, Debrecen, Oradea, Cluj-Napoca, Iași, Timișoara, Arad, Sibiu, Brașov, Ploiești, Craiova, Galați, Constanța, Novi Sad, Sarajevo, Varna

West from / East from Greenwich

CARTOGRAPHY BY PHILIP'S. COPYRIGHT REED INTERNATIONAL BOOKS LTD

Grid columns (bottom): 9 10 11 12 13 14 15

Projection: Conical with two standard parallels

U r a l

URAL

Bolshezemelskaya Tundra

Malozemelskaya Tundra

G. of Pechora

Kolguyev

Kanin Pen.

Chesha B.

C. Kanin Nos

Rybachi Pen.

Kola B.

Murmansk

Monchegorsk

Imandra L.

Kandalaksha

Kandalaksha G.

KOLA PEN.

White Sea

Kola Pen.

Lapland

NORWAY

SWEDEN

Bodø

Mo

Kebnekaise 2117

Kiruna

Gällivare

Torne L.

Torne

Kalix

Luleå

Piteå

Umeå

Gulf of Bothnia

Åland Is. (Ahvenanmaa)

Stockholm

Soderhamn

Sundsvall

Angerman

Inari L.

Kemijärvi

Kemi

Rovaniemi

Oulu

Kuopio

FINLAND

Vaasa

Pori

Turku

Tampere

Lahti

Helsinki

Kotka

Hanko

Viborg

Saimaa

Savonlinna

Sortavala

Priozersk

L. Ladoga

Petrozavodsk

Olonets

Medvezhyegorsk

KARELIA

Belomorsk

Top L.

Pya L.

Kuito Ls.

Segozero

Povenets

L. Vyg

Kem

Onega

Dvina B.

Severodvinsk

Arkhangelsk

Onega

Pechora

Ust Usa

Ust Tsilma

Naryan-Mar

Vorkuta

Kholmer Yu 1363

Labytnangi

Salekhard

Narodnaya 1894

Telposiz 1617

Inta

Usa

Intu

Pechora

Troitsko-Pechorsk

Ukhta

Sosnogorsk

Zheleznodorozhny

Syktyvkar

Koslan

Mikun

Vym

Vychegda

Velsky Ustyug

Kotlas

Pinyug

Mezen

Mezen

Karpogory

Pinega

Plesetsk

Nyandoma

Konosha

Vologda

Totma

Velsk

Kholmogorsk

Vyatka

Kirov

Slobodskoy

Glazov

UDMURTIA

Izhevsk

Votkinsk

Sarapul

Kama

Yekaterinburg

Sverdlovsk

Nizhniy Tagil 1569

Krasnoturinsk

Serov

Ivdel

Kizel

Berezniki

Solikamsk

Chusovoy

Lysva

Kungur

PERM

Kama

Nolinsk

Yoshkar-Ola

MARI EL

Cheboksary

CHUVASHIA

KAZAN

TATARSTAN

Volga

Zelenodolsk

Alatyr

Kuznetsk 351

Syzran

Volsk

Balakovo

SAMARA (Kuybyshev)

Togliatti Kuybyshev Reservoir

Novokuybyshevsk

Dimitrovgrad

Bugulma

Naberezhnyye Chelny

Birsk

BASHKORTOSTAN

UFA

Belaya

Chernikovsk

Sterlitamak

Salavat

Yaman-Tau 1640

Zlatoust

Miass

Beloretsk

Magnitogorsk

Orsk

Novotroitsk

Orenburg

Buzuluk

Sorochinsk

Buguruslan

Penza

MORDVINIA

Saransk

Serdobsk

Tambov

Morshansk

Arzamas

Dzerzhinsk

Gorki Reservoir

Nizhniy Novgorod Gorki

Murom

Vladimir

Orekhovo-Zuyevo

Ivanovo

Kineshma

Kostroma

Yaroslavl

Rybinsk

Rybinsk Reservoir

Cherepovets

Belozersk

Beloye L.

Kargopol

Kondopoga L. Onega

Vytegra

Lodeynoye Pole

Novaya Ladoga

L. Onega

Podporozhye

L. Ilmen

Staraya Russa

Novgorod

ST. PETERSBURG Leningrad

Narva

Luga

Lugo

ESTONIA

Tallinn

Pärnu

Hiiumaa

Saaremaa

G. of Riga

Ventspils

Liepaja

Klaipeda

Sovetsk

Kaliningrad

(RUSSIA)

LITHUANIA

Kaunas

Vilnius

Šiauliai

Jelgava

LATVIA

Riga

Daugavpils

Daugava

Pskov

Chudskoye L.

Tartu

Velikaya

BELARUS

MINSK

Baranovichi

Bobruysk

Borisov

Berezina

Grodno

Brest

Pinsk

Pripet Marshes

Pripet

Niemen

POLAND

WARSAW

Lublin

Bialystok

Lomza

Bug

Chernigov

Gomel

Mogilev

Orsha

Vitebsk

Smolensk

Roslavl

Bryansk

Orel

Kursk

Dnieper

Dnepr

Desna

VALDAI HILLS

Valdai Hills

Vyshniy Volochek

Tver

Rzhev

Vyazma

Velikiye Luki

Borovichi

Volga

RUSSIA

MOSCOW

Moskva

Sergiyev Posad

Podolsk

Serpukhov

Kaluga

Tula

Novomoskovsk

Orekhovo-Zuyevo

Kolomna

Ryazan

Michurinsk

Lipetsk

Yelets

Arctic Circle

1 : 50 000 000

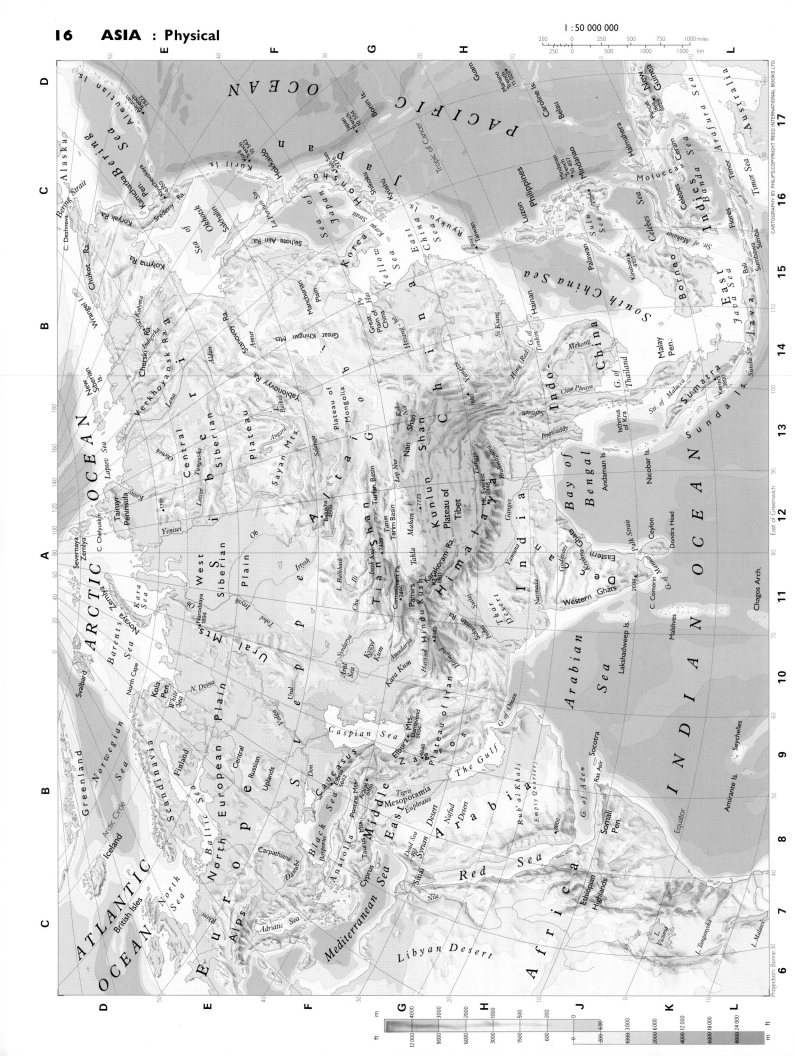

CARTOGRAPHY BY PHILIPS. COPYRIGHT REED INTERNATIONAL BOOKS LTD.

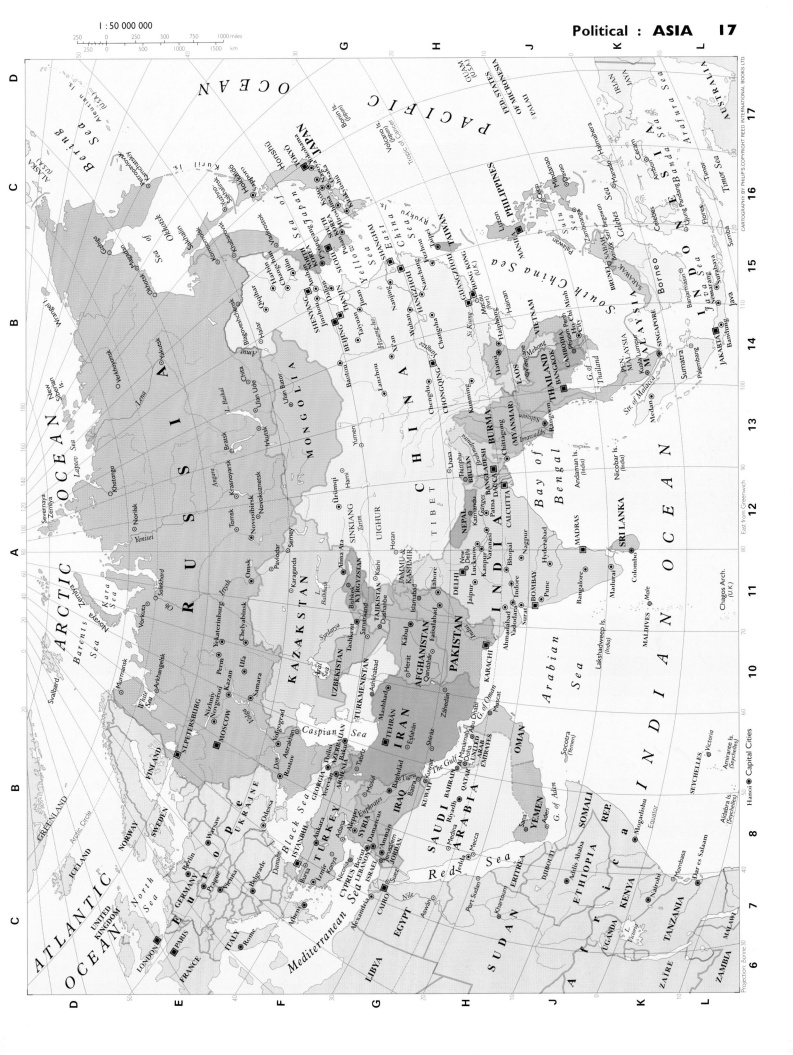

1 : 50 000 000

250   0   250   500   750   1000 miles
250   0   500   1000   1500   km

PACIFIC OCEAN

ARCTIC OCEAN

ATLANTIC OCEAN

INDIAN OCEAN

R U S S I A

C H I N A

K A Z A K S T A N

MONGOLIA

I N D I A

I N D O N E S I A

A F R I C A

Bering Sea

Sea of Okhotsk

Sea of Japan

Yellow Sea

East China Sea

South China Sea

Java Sea

Bay of Bengal

Arabian Sea

Caspian Sea

Red Sea

Black Sea

Mediterranean Sea

Barents Sea

Kara Sea

Laptev Sea

Banda Sea

Timor Sea

Arafura Sea

JAPAN
TOKYO

PHILIPPINES
MANILA

MONGOLIA
Ulan Bator

BEIJING
SHENYANG

SEOUL
N. KOREA
S. KOREA
PYONGYANG

TAIWAN

SHANGHAI

GUANGZHOU
HONG KONG (U.K.)

VIETNAM
Hanoi

LAOS
Vientiane

THAILAND
BANGKOK

CAMBODIA
Phnom Penh
Ho Chi Minh City

BURMA
(MYANMAR)
Rangoon

MALAYSIA
Kuala Lumpur
SINGAPORE

BRUNEI
SABAH
SARAWAK
Borneo

JAKARTA
Bandung

SRI LANKA
Colombo

INDIA
New Delhi
DELHI
CALCUTTA
BOMBAY
MADRAS
Bangalore
Hyderabad

NEPAL
BHUTAN
BANGLADESH
DACCA

PAKISTAN
KARACHI
Islamabad
Lahore

AFGHANISTAN
Kābul
Qandahār
Herāt

IRAN
TEHRĀN
Eşfahān
Shīrāz

IRAQ
Baghdād
Basra

SAUDI ARABIA
Riyadh
Mecca
Medina

YEMEN
Sana

OMAN
Muscat

U.A.E.
Abu Dhabi

QATAR
BAHRAIN
KUWAIT

TURKEY
ISTANBUL
Ankara

SYRIA
Damascus
Aleppo

LEBANON
Beirut
ISRAEL
Jerusalem
JORDAN
Amman

CYPRUS
Nicosia

EGYPT
CAIRO

GEORGIA
Tbilisi
ARMENIA
Yerevan
AZERBAIJAN
Baku

UZBEKISTAN
Tashkent
Samarkand
TURKMENISTAN
Ashkhabad
TAJIKISTAN
Dushanbe
KYRGYZSTAN
Bishkek

MOSCOW
S.PETERSBURG

SAINT PETERSBURG

FINLAND
NORWAY
SWEDEN
UKRAINE
GERMANY
E u r o p e

UNITED KINGDOM
LONDON
FRANCE
PARIS
ITALY
Rome

SUDAN
ETHIOPIA
SOMALI REP.
Mogadishu
KENYA
Nairobi
TANZANIA
UGANDA
ZAIRE

SINKIANG
UIGHUR
TIBET
Lhasa

AUSTRALIA

FED. STATES OF MICRONESIA

GUAM (USA)

East from Greenwich

Projection Bonne 30

Hanoi ⊙ Capital Cities

Tropic of Cancer

Arctic Circle

Equator

1 : 35 000 000

200 0 200 400 600 800 miles

400 0 400 800 1200 km

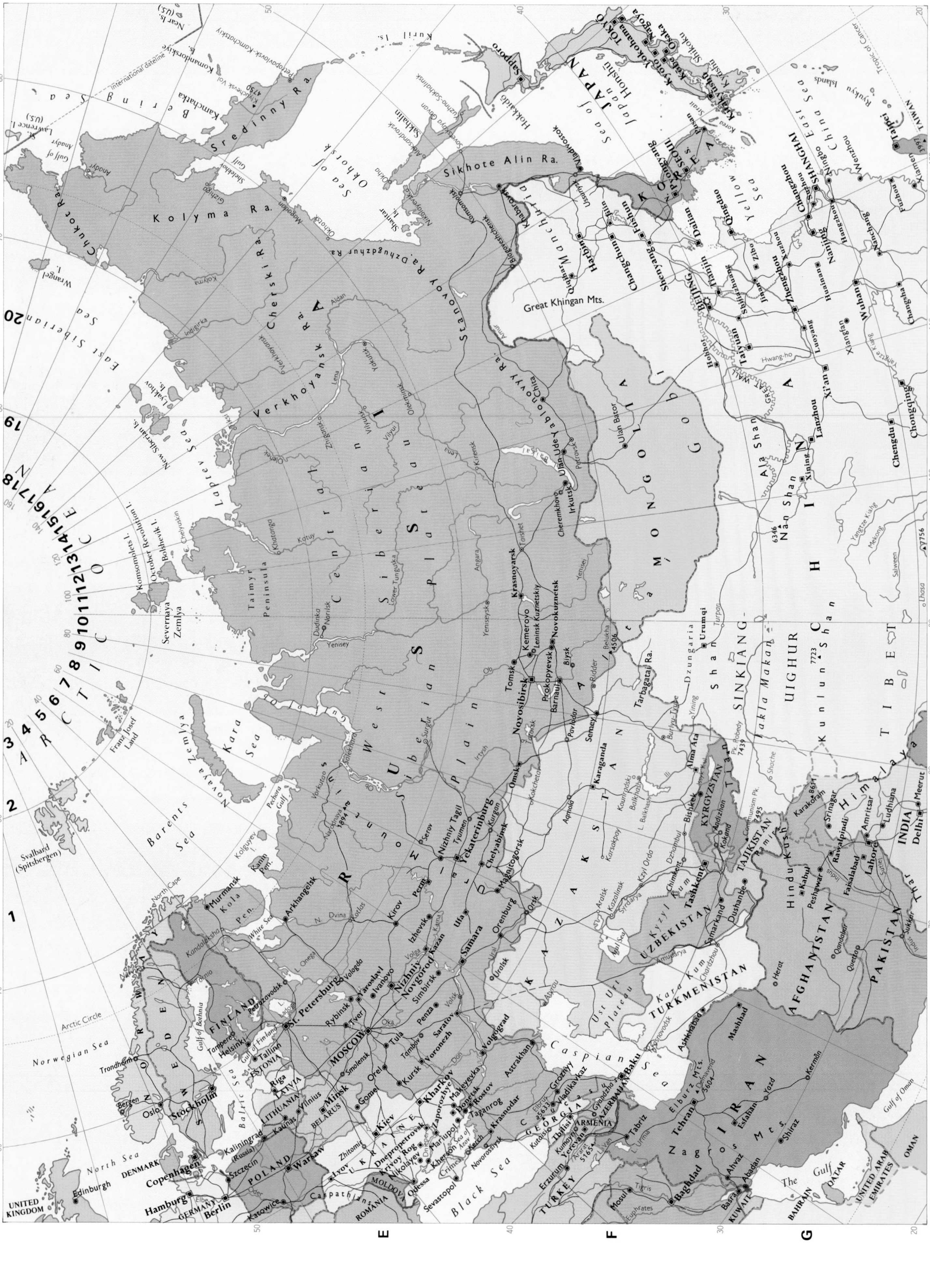

ARCTIC OCEAN
Barents Sea
Kara Sea
Laptev Sea
East Siberian Sea
Bering Sea
Sea of Okhotsk
Sea of Japan
Yellow Sea
East China Sea
Norwegian Sea
North Sea
Baltic Sea
Black Sea
Caspian Sea
Aral Sea
The Gulf
Gulf of Oman
Svalbard (Spitsbergen)
Franz Josef Land
Novaya Zemlya
Severnaya Zemlya
Taimyr Peninsula
New Siberian Is.
Wrangel I.
Sakhalin
Kuril Is.
Hokkaido
Honshu
Kyushu
Shikoku
RUSSIA
West Siberian Plain
Central Siberian Plateau
Verkhoyansk Ra.
Cherski Ra.
Kolyma Ra.
Chukot Ra.
Sredinny Ra.
Stanovoy Ra.
Dzhugdzhur Ra.
Sikhote Alin Ra.
Yablonovy Ra.
Ural Mts.
Great Khingan Mts.
Caucasus
Elburz Mts.
Zagros Mts.
Hindu Kush
Himalaya
Kunlun Shan
Tien Shan
Nan Shan
Altai
Gobi
Takla Makan
Kara Kum
Kyzyl Kum
Ust Urt Plateau
FINLAND
SWEDEN
NORWAY
DENMARK
UNITED KINGDOM
GERMANY
POLAND
ESTONIA
LATVIA
LITHUANIA
BELARUS
UKRAINE
MOLDOVA
ROMANIA
TURKEY
GEORGIA
ARMENIA
AZERBAIJAN
KAZAKSTAN
UZBEKISTAN
TURKMENISTAN
KYRGYZSTAN
TAJIKISTAN
AFGHANISTAN
PAKISTAN
INDIA
IRAN
KUWAIT
BAHRAIN
QATAR
UNITED ARAB EMIRATES
OMAN
MONGOLIA
CHINA
SINKIANG UIGHUR
TIBET
KOREA
JAPAN
TAIWAN
MOSCOW
St. Petersburg
Novosibirsk
Yekaterinburg
Omsk
Krasnoyarsk
Irkutsk
Ulan Ude
Chita
Khabarovsk
Vladivostok
Yakutsk
Magadan
Petropavlovsk-Kamchatskiy
Murmansk
Arkhangelsk
Nizhniy Novgorod
Kazan
Samara
Volgograd
Kiev
Minsk
Tashkent
Alma Ata
Bishkek
Dushanbe
Ashkhabad
Tehran
Baghdad
Kabul
Delhi
Lahore
Ulan Bator
BEIJING
SHANGHAI
TOKYO
SEOUL
P'yongyang
Urumqi
Lhasa
Arctic Circle
Tropic of Cancer
International dateline
East from Greenwich

Projection: Lambert's Conical Orthomorphic

1   2   3   4   5

50

K A Z A K S T A N

Karaganda
Karsakpay
70
1565
Karkaralinsk
Rubtsovsk
Semey
Oskeman
80
R
Western Sayan
Tannu Ola
Munku Sardyk 3491
Cheremkhovo
Angarsk
Irkutsk
90
455
U S S I A

B

342 Lake Balkhash
Ayaguz
Lake Zaisan
Belukha 4506
Zyryanovsk
Fuhai
Fuyun
Altay
Uvs Nuur
Hovd
Har Us Nuur
Ulaangom
Hyargas Nuur
Döröö Nuur
Ulyasutay
Khangai
Selenge Moron
Orhon Gol
Tsetserleg
Altanbulag
Dzuunmod
Ulan Bator

Taldy-Kurgan
Chu
Ala Tau
Tacheng
Ala Kul
Karamay
A l t a i
4362
M O N G O
Buyanhongor
Dzuunmod

Bishkek
Dzhambul
Issyk-Kul
1609
Alma Ata
Yining
Ili
Bole
Dzungarian Gates
Usu
Karamay
D z u n g a r i a n
Qitai
Tsetserleg
Dalandzadgad

KYRGYZSTAN
Namangan
Andizhan
Naryn
T
Pik Pobedy
7439
Aksu
Kuqa
Korla
Bosten (Bagrax) Hu
Ürümqi 5445
Turpan -154
Hami
4925
Gaxun Nur
G
o

40

Kashi
S I N K I A N G
U I G H U R
Kuruktag
Tarim He
T a r i m   B a s i n
Lop Nor
Dunhuang
Anxi
Yumen
Jiayuguan
Ala Shan
Linhe
Wuhai 2514

Shache
T a k l a   M a k a n
1635
Yecheng
Hotan
Yutian
Qiemo
Ruoqiang
Altun Shan
N a n
6346
Zhangye
G
Alxa Zuoqi
NINGXIA
Yinchuan
HUIZU

Karakoram
K2 8611
8126
JAMMU &
KASHMIR
Srinagar
Leh
Karakoram Pass
5575
7723
K u n - l u n
Da Qaidam
Qaidam-pendi
Golmud
Dulan
S h a n
Tianjun
Qinghai Hu 3205
Gonghe
QINGHAI
Xining
Wuwei
Wuzhong
ZIZHIQU

C

Rutog
Gar
T I B E T
T a n g l h a   R a n g e
Amdo
Ngoring Hu 4237
Gyaring Hu
Yushu
B a y a n   H a r   S h a n
Maqen
6094
Min Xian
LANZHOU
Linxia
Pingliang
Tianshui
Baoji
C
H

Nanda Devi 7817
Dehra Dun
Burang
Mapam Yumco
Zhongba
Xainza
Siling Co 4495
Nam Co 4627
Nagqu
Qamdo
Mekong
Ning Shan
Shaluli Shan
Garze
Daxue Shan
Min
Wudu
Hanzhong
4113
Jialing

30

Meerut
DELHI
Moradabad
Bareilly
Aligarh
Agra
Ghaghra
Dhaulagiri 8221
N E P A L
Katmandu
Gorakhpur
H i m
a
l
Lhaze
Xigaze
Xainza
Yamzho Yumco
Lhasa
Namcha Barwa 7756
Bomi
Yangtze (Jinsha)
Salween (Nu Jiang)
Zayü
5881
Zhongdian
Xichang
Lijiang
Mianyang
Daxian
S I C H U A N
CHENGDU
Neijiang
Zigong
Luzhou
Yibin
Wutongqiao
Gogga Shan 7600
Dadu
Nanchong
Hechuan
CHONG
(Chongx)
Zunyi
Wu

D

KANPUR
Gwalior
LUCKNOW
Jhansi
I N D I A
Allahabad
Patna
Varanasi
Everest 8848
a
l
a
y
a
Koch Bihar
BHUTAN
Thimphu
Brahmaputra
Dibrugarh
Gauhati
Tezpur
Patkai Hills
3411
Myitkyina
Zhonghian
Daliang Shan
Zhaotong
Dongchuan
GUIZHO
Guiyang
Zhanyi
Anshun

Tropic of Cancer
Jabalpur
Ranchi
Jamshedpur
Rajshahi
BANGLADESH
Khasi Hills
Khulna
Haora
CALCUTTA
Silchar
Imphal 3824
Bhamo
Luxi
Baoshan
BURMA
Xiaguan
KUNMING
Xingyi
Duyun
Hechi
GUA

20

Raipur
NAGPUR
80
Cuttack
Mahanadi
Indravati
BAY OF
BENGAL
Akyab
CHITTAGONG
Arakan Yoma
Victoria 3053
Monywa
Chindwin
(MYANMAR)
Mandalay
2650
Irrawaddy
Pegu Yoma
Y U N N A N
Shiping
Gejiu
Wenshan
Jiangcheng
3143
VIETNAM
Pingxiang
Nanning
ZIZ
Qinzhou

E

Warangal
Vishakhapatnam
Narayanganj
DACCA (Dhaka)
Yamethin
Toungoo
Salween
2763
THAILAND
Luang Prabang
LAOS
Mekong
Hoa-Binh
HANOI
HAIPHONG
Gulf of Tonkin

Projection: Bonne   3   90   4   100   East from Greenwich   5

1 : 15 000 000

100   0   100   200   300   400 miles
100   0   100   200   300   400   500   600 km

6   **8**

Lake Baykal
Ulan Ude   ● Chita   Nerchinsk   Svobodny   ○ Chegdomyn   Aleksandrovsk   C. Terpeniya

Sakhalin

Hentiyn Nuruu   Yablonovyy Range   Borzya   Blagoveshchensk   Amur   L. Bolon   Komsomolsk   Poronaysk

L I A   Manzhouli   Orogen Zizhiqi   Aihui   Birobidzhan   Khabarovsk   Yuzhno-Sakhalinsk

Hulun Nur   Hailar   Bei'an   Yichun   Hegang   Jiamusi   Bikin   La Perouse Str.

Choybalsan   Butha Qi   Qiqihar   Anda   Suihua   Shuangyashan   Mishan   Wakkanai   B

Kerulen   Buir Nur   Nenjiang   Jixi   Lake Khanka   Asahigawa   2290   Kushiro

Saynshand   Horqin Youyi Qianqi   HARBIN   Ussuriysk   Sikhote Alin Ra.   Otaru   HOKKAIDO

Abagnar Qi   Tao'an   Mudanjiang   Vladivostok   SAPPORO   C. Erimo

Dzamin Üüd   Erenhot   1949   CHANGCHUN   Jilin   Nakhodka   Hakodate   Tsugaru Strait   Aomori   Hachinohe

INNER MONGOLIA   Shuangliao   Siping   Songhua Lake   Yanji   Akita   Morioka

Tongliao   Liaoyuan   2744   Chongjin   SEA OF   Sado   Sendai

Hohhot   Chifeng   FUSHUN   NORTH   Niigata   Utsunomiya

Baotou   Datong   Jining   Zhangjiakou   SHENYANG   Tonghua   Hungnam   JAPAN   Toyama   Kanazawa   TOKYO

Ordos   Xuanhua   Chaoyang   Liaoyang   Benxi   KOREA   Wŏnsan   KAWASAKI   YOKOHAMA

Us   Qinhuangdao   Yingkou   ANSHAN   Dandong   PYONGYANG   NAGOYA   Fuji-san   Yokosuka   C

mo   GREAT WALL   3058   BEIJING   G. of Liaodong   Yalu   DALIAN   Haeju   Kaesong   KYOTO   KOBE   OSAKA   Shizuoka

TAIYUAN   HEBEI   Tangshan   Liaodong Pen.   Korea Bay   SEOUL   Okayama   Sakai   Hamamatsu

Baoding   TIANJIN (Tientsin)   G. of Chihli   Bo Hai   INCHON   Wakayama

Yangquan   Shijiazhuang   Cangzhou   Yantai   Weihai   SOUTH   Hiroshima   Shikoku   Kochi

Fenyang   Yuci   Dezhou   JINAN   Weifang   Taejon   TAEGU   PUSAN   Matsuyama

Changzhi   Handan   Zibo   Tai'an   QINGDAO   KITAKYUSHU   Kumamoto

Tongchuan   Anyang   Jining   YELLOW   Kwangju   Masan   FUKUOKA   Kyushu

Sanmenxia   Xinxiang   Lanyungang   SEA   1915   Shimonoseki   Sasebo   Kumamoto

XIAN (Sian)   ZHENGZHOU   Kaifeng   Cheju Do   Nagasaki   Kagoshima

HENAN   Pingdingshan   Xuzhou   Qingjiang   JIANGSU   T950   J

Nanyang   Shangqiu   Shangshui   Honghu Hu   Changzhou   Nantong   Tanega

Ankang   Han Shui   Zhumadian   Bengbu   NANJING (Nanking)   Zhenjiang   Wuxi   SHANGHAI

Xiangfan   Dabie Shan   Huainan   ANHUI   Hefei   Wuhu   Suzhou   EAST CHINA

HUBEI   WUHAN   Tongling   Hangzhou   Hangzhou Wan

Yichang   Shashi   Huangshi   Anqing   Yangtze   Shaoxing   Ningbo   SEA   Amami-ō-Shima

Changde   Jiujiang   ZHEJIANG   Jinhua   Ryukyu Islands

Dongting L.   Nanchang   Poyang L.   Shangrao   Jingdezhen   Wenzhou

Yiyang   Changsha   JIANGXI   Wu Shan   2120   Okinawa   D

HUNAN   Xiangtan   Zhuzhou   Jian   Naha

Shaoyang   Hengyang   Nanping   Sakishima Gunto

Nan Ling   Sanming   Fuzhou   FUJIAN   PACIFIC

Guilin   Shaoguan   Ganzhou   Quanzhou   Chilung   Tropic of Cancer

Zhangzhou   TAIPEI   Taichung

Wuzhou   Mei Xian   Xiamen (Amoy)   Chao'an   Chiai   Yu Shan   3997   TAIWAN

GUANGDONG   Foshan   GUANGZHOU (Canton)   Shantou   Tainan   OCEAN

Maoming   Jiangmen   HONG KONG (U.K.)   KAOHSIUNG   E

Zhanjiang   Macau (Port.)   Batan Is.   20

SOUTH CHINA   Babuyan Is.

Haikou   SEA   COPYRIGHT GEORGE PHILIP & SON LTD

HAINAN   1879

6   **120**   **7**   **130**   **8**

1 : 20 000 000

100   0   100   200   300   400 miles
100   0   100   200   300   400   500   600 km

Projection: Bonne

East from Greenwich

COPYRIGHT GEORGE PHILIP & SON, LTD

PACIFIC   OCEAN

CHINA

TAIWAN

HONG KONG (U.K.)
Macau (Port.)

Zhanjiang
Haikou
Hainan

BURMA (MYANMAR)

Yamethin
Taunggyi
Toungoo
RANGOON
Bassein
Moulmein
Ramree
Cheduba I.
Pt. Blair
Mouths of Irrawaddy
G. of Martaban

Middle Andaman
Andaman Islands (India)
Little Andaman

Mergui
Mergui Arch.

ANDAMAN   SEA

Ten Degree Channel
Car Nicobar
Great Nicobar
Nicobar Islands (India)

LAOS
VIET-NAM
Hanoi
Haiphong
Nam Dinh
G. of Tongking
Thanh Hoa
Vinh
Ha Tinh
Quang Tri
Hue
Da Nang
An Nhon
Qui Nhon
Nha Trang
Phan Rang
Phan Thiet
Luang Prabang
Vientiane
Udon Thani
Phu Loi
Phitsanulok
Uttaradit
Chiengmai
Tak

THAILAND (SIAM)
Nakhon Ratchasima
Ubon
Pakse
BANGKOK
Ayutthaya
Chanthaburi
Srepok
Kratié
Phnom Dangrek
Tonle Sap
Battambang
CAMBODIA
Phnom Penh
Kg. Cham
Kg. Chhnang
Kg. Thom
Kompong Som
Long Xuyen
HO CHI MINH CITY
Bien Hoa
Go Cong
Can Tho

Gulf of Thailand

Chumphon
Isthmus of Kra
Nakhon Si Thammarat
Songkhla
Phuket
Trang

SOUTH   CHINA   SEA

Paracel Is.

PHILIPPINE

Batan Is.
Bashi Channel
Babuyan Is.
Babuyan Chan.
LUZON
Laoag
Aparri
Baguio
Quezon City
MANILA
Lamon B.
Polillo Is.
Mindoro
Calamian Group
Calapan
Tablas
Masbate
Panay
Iloilo
Negros
Cebu
Bacolod
Bohol
Ozamiz
Mindanao
Zamboanga
Basilan
Jolo
Davao
Cagayan
Butuan
Surigao Strait
San Bernardino Str.
Samar
Tacloban
Leyte
C. S. Agustin
Moro Gulf
Sarangani B.
Tinaca Point

SULU   SEA
SULU
Balabac Str.
Palawan
Kudat
Kota Kinabalu
Kinabalu 4101
Labuan
SABAH
Sandakan
Tawau
Tarakan
Brassey Ra.
Banggi

BRUNEI
Bandar Seri Begawan
Miri

SARAWAK
Sibu
Kuching
Schwaner Ra.
Muller Ra.
Kapuas Hulu Ra.
Iran or Tamo Ra.

MALAYSIA
Natuna Is.
S. Natuna
Anambas Is.
Kota Baharu
Kuala Terengganu
G. Tahan 2190
Kuala Lumpur
Seremban
Melaka
Johor Baharu
SINGAPORE
Butterworth
Taiping
Ipoh
Telok Anson
Port Kelang
Muar
Rupat
Bengkalis
George Town
Penang
Strait of Malacca

Riau Arch.
Lingga
Bintan
Berhala Str.
Pontianak
KALIMANTAN
Pangkalpinang
Bangka
Beliton
Karimata
Kuala Kapuas
Banjarmasin
Barito
Balikpapan
Mahakam
Little Laut
Laut I.

INDONESIA
Medan
Tebingtinggi
Pematangsiantar
Toba
Sibolga
Padang
Sawahlunto
Jambi
Palembang
Telukbetun
Pekanbaru
Bukittinggi
Kerinci 3800
Padang
Mentawai Is.
Siberut
Sipora
N. Pagai
S. Pagai
Enggano
Bengkulu
Musi

Nias
Batu Is.
Banyak Is.
Simeulue
Banda Aceh

SUMATRA

JAVA SEA
Bawean
Karimunjawa
JAKARTA
Bogor
Bandung
Cirebon
Tegal
Pekalongan
Semarang
Magelang
Surakarta
Yogyakarta
Madiun
Kediri
Malang
SURABAYA
Madura
JAVA
Cilacap
3426

Bali
Denpasar
Lombok
Sumbawa
Kangean Is.
3726
FLORES SEA
Flores
Sumba
Rinca
Ruteng
Sawu
Waingapu
Maumere
TIMOR
Kupang
Dili
Wetar
Alor
Pantar
Lombien
Ombai Str.

CELEBES   SEA
Sangihe
Talaud Is.
Manado
Gorontalo
G. of Tomini
SULAWESI (Celebes)
Rantepao 3455
Pare-pare
Ujung Pandang (Makasar)
Kendari
Butung
Selayar
Str. of Makasar

Morotai
Halmahera
Ternate
Obi Is.
Peleng
Banggai Arch.
Taliabu
Mangole
Sula Is.
Buru
Ceram
Ambon
Banda Is.
Gebe

MOLUCCA SEA
Moluccas

CERAM   SEA

BANDA   SEA
Tanimbar Is.
Leti Is.
Kai Is.
Aru Is.
Tanahdena
Yamdena
Selaru

IRIAN JAYA
Biak
Yapen
Manokwari
Vogelkop
Sorong
Misool
Waigeo
Wokam
Kobroor
Trangan

ARAFURA   SEA

TIMOR   SEA
Melville I.
Bathurst I.
Wessel Is.
C. Arnhem
G. Van Diemen
Darwin
AUSTRALIA

INDIAN   OCEAN

Christmas I. (Austral.)
Cocos or Keeling Is. (Austral.)

Equator

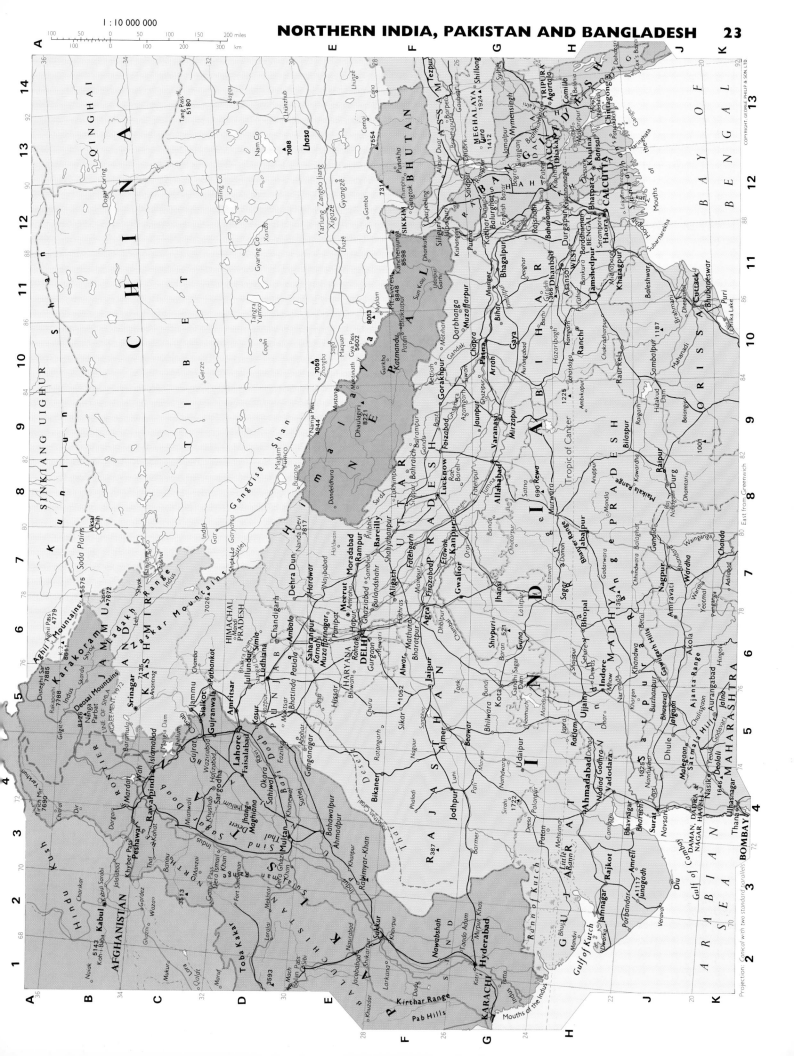

1 2 3 4 5

B

KAZAKHSTAN
KAZAK
Borisovka

TURKEY
Konya Kayseri Malatya Erzurum Yerevan Kumayri Gyandzha ARMENIA AZERBAIJAN Baku
Antalya Taurus Mersin Adana Elâziğ Mus Van Bitlis Araks Kara Bogaz Gol Krasnovodsk Urgench UZBEKISTAN Samar
Gaziantep Diyarbakir Kurdistan Urmia Tabriz Lenkoran Caspian Sea TURKMENISTAN Bukhara
CYPRUS Nicosia Aleppo (Halab) Latakia Mosul Erbil Urmia Ardabil Anzali Rasht Babol Kum Karshi Chardzhou
LEBANON Tripoli Hama SYRIA Euphrates Zanjan Qazvin Elburz Mountains Ashkhabad Bairam-Ali Kerki Terme
Beirut Homs Mesopotamia Kirkuk Tehran Damavend 5604 Ernamrud Mashhad Mary Mazar-e Sharif
Alexandria Damanhur Mansura Haifa ISRAEL Tel Aviv Damascus IRAQ Bakhtaran Hamadan Qom Maimana Herat
Dumyât Jaffa Jerusalem Ar Ramadi Araq Kashan Tabas AFGHANISTAN
Tanta Ismailia Port Said JORDAN Amman Karbala Baghdad Esfahan Yazd Birjan Ghazn
Cairo Suez Dead Sea Al Kut Hilla 4548 Farah Farah Kab
El Faiyum Sinai 2637 Ma'an An Najaf An Nâsiriyah Ahvaz Shiraz 4075 Anar Dasht-e Lut Girishko Qandahar

C

Luxor Qena Bûr Safâga Al Jawf Nafud Desert Ahvaz Khorramshahr Abadan KUWAIT Kuwait Bandar Khomeyni Kazerun Kerman Zahedan Helmand Nushki Quetta
Qusêir W. Hamd Hail Turabah Shatt al Arab Busehr Jahrom Saidabad Bam PAKIS
Ras Banas Al'Ula Burâydah Al Qatif The Gulf Bandar Abbas Central Makran Ra. Shikarpur
Yenbo Medina HEJAZ SAUDI Dammam BAHRAIN Str. of Hormuz Jask Dasht
Yâbigh Arif Riyadh Mubarraz Al-Hufuf QATAR Doha Sharjah Dubai Gwadar Ormara Karachi Indus Delta
SUDAN Halaib Jedda Mecca ARABIA Abu Dhabi As Sohar Gulf of Oman Pasni G.
Taif UNITED ARAB EMIRATES Hajar Tropic of Cancer Nawabshah
Port Sudan Layla 3048 Muscat
Suakin Sulaiyil Ras al Hadd

D

'Asir Rub' al Khali OMAN G. of Masirah
Mesewa Abha (Empty Quarter) Ras al Madraka
Asmera ERITREA Amram Kuria Muria Is.
Al Hudaydah Sana' Shibam Mirbat
Dahlak Arch. Farasan Is. Yarim Hadhramaut Ras Fartak
116 Ta'izz YEMEN Sayhut Ras Fartak ARABIAN
Dese Mussa Ali 2063 Bab el Mandeb Shuqra Mukalla
DJIBOUTI Aden Madinat al Shaab Gulf of Aden SEA
Dire Dawa Djibouti Socotra (Yemen)
Harar Berbera Ras Asir (C. Guardafui)
ETHIOPIA Hargeisa Erigavo
Ogaden Hordio
Gabredarre SOMALI REP. Bender Beila
Juba Ilig
Shibeli Obbia Mogadishu

INDIA

1:17 500 000

100 0 100 200 300 400 500 miles
100 0 100 200 300 400 500 600 700 800 km

KYRGYZSTAN
Alma Ata
Dzhambul
Chimkent Bishkek
Namangan
Tashkent
Andizhan
Kokand
Fergana
Khodzent
TAJIKISTAN
7495
shanbe Pamirs
Faizabad
Kush
Chitral
Gilgit
Karakoram
K2
8611
HIM.
PRAD.
JAMMU AND
KASHMIR
Leh
Khyber
Pass
Peshawar
Islamabad Srinagar
Rawalpindi
Jammu
Sialkot
Gujranwala
Lahore Amritsar
Jullunder
Faisalabad PUNJAB Ludhiana
Ambala
Sahiwal Ratiala
Multan
Bahawalpur
HARYANA
Meerut
Delhi
Bikaner
Jaipur
Jodhpur
RAJASTHAN
Beawar Ajmer
Udaipur
Mandsaur
Palanpur
Ahmadabad
Vadodara
Bharuch
Rajkot
Bhavnagar
Surat
Thana
Bombay
Pune
Sangli
Kolhapur
Panjim
GOA
Mangalore

SINKIANG UIGHUR
Tarim
Takla Makan
Kashi
Shache
Hotan
Kuruk tag
Lop Nur
Bosten Hu
Pk. Pobedy
7439
Issyk Kul
Tarim Basin
Altun Shan
7723
Kun Lun Shan
Gar
TIBET
Maquan He
Xigaze
Lhasa
Nam
Co
Nyainqen tanglha Shan
Ta Tanggula Shan
CHINA
QINGHAI
Qaidam Pendi
Golmud
Qaidam He
Gyaring
Hu
Petinho
Qinghai Hu
Yumen
Nan Shan
6346
Xining
Lanzhou
Linxia
Pingliang
Tanggula
Shankou
5180
Yushu
Qamdo
Mekong
Garze
Yangtze
Chengdu
SICHUAN
Chongqing
Yibin
Kunming
YUNNAN
Xiaguan
Tengchong
Gejiu
Mekong
Wuwei
Huang He
Tianshui
Hanzhong
Baoji
Xi'an
Wei

NEPAL
Dhaulagiri
8221
Mt. Everest
8848
Katmandu
SIKKIM
Darjeeling
Gorakhpur
Darbhanga
BHUTAN
ARUNACHAL PRADESH
Mebu
Sadiya
Tezpur
NAGALAND
Brahmaputra
Dehra Dun
Hardwar
Moradabad
Rampur
Bareilly
Shahjahanpur
Aligarh
UTTAR
Mathura
Agra
PRADESH
Lucknow
Etawah
Kanpur
Jaunpur
Chapra
Patna
Arrah
Gwalior
Jhansi
Allahabad
Varanasi
Mirzapur
Ganges
Bhagalpur
Gaya
Dhanbad
BIHAR
Ranchi
Jamshedpur
Bhopal
MADHYA
Ujjain
Indore
PRADESH
Jabalpur
Bilaspur
Vindhya Range
Satpura Range
Indravati
NAGPUR
Raipur
Amravati
Akola
ORISSA
Mahanadi
Cuttack
Bhubaneswar
Puri
Berhampur
Dhule
Jalna
Nasik
Godavari
Nanded
Nizamabad
Ahmadnagar
Warangal
Solapur
Gulbarga
Bhima
Hyderabad
Bijapur
Krishna
DECCAN
Belgaum
Dharwad
Gadag
Adoni
Kurnool
Bellary
KARNATAKA
Davangere
Shimoga
Kolar
Bangalore
Mysore
Vellore
Kottagudam
Godavari
Rajahmundry
Kakinada
Eluru
Vijayawada
Guntur
Nellore
Vishaknapatnam

MEGHALAYA
TRIPURA
MIZO
RAM
Lushai
Hills
MANIPUR
Imphal
BANGLADESH
Dacca
Khulna
Barisal
Chittagong
Sundarbans
BENGAL
Calcutta
Kharagpur
Myitkyina
Lashio
Mandalay
Kyaukse
Myingyan
Shwebo
BURMA
(MYANMAR)
Arakan Yoma
Minbu
Pegu Yoma
2676
Yamethin
Chindwin
Irrawaddy
LAOS
THAILAND
Chiengmai
Uttaradit
Tak
Salween
Ping
Nan
Mekong
Hou

Bay
of
Bengal

Coromandel Coast

Andaman
Islands
(India)
Port Blair
Lit. Andaman
Andaman
Sea
Ten Degree Channel
Mergui
Archipelago
Tavoy
Tenasserim
Bilauk Taung Ra
Moulmein
Rangoon
Yè
G. of
Martaban
Bassein
C. Negrais
Sittwe

Madras
Pondicherry
Salem
TAMIL
Kumbakonam
NADU
Tiruchchirappalli
Palghat
2698
Anai Mudi
Coimbatore
Calicut
Cochin
Mattancheri
Quilon
Trivandrum
Nagercoil
C. Comorin
KERALA
Tuticorin
Tirunelveli
Puttalam
Mannar
Jaffna
Trincomalee
SRI LANKA
Batticaloa
Kandy
Pidurutalagala
2524
Colombo
Galle
Dondra
Head
G. of Mannar

Lakshadweep Is.
(India)

Malabar Coast

Nicobar
Islands
(India)
Great Channel
Banda Aceh
INDONESIA
Simeulue

MALDIVES
OCEAN

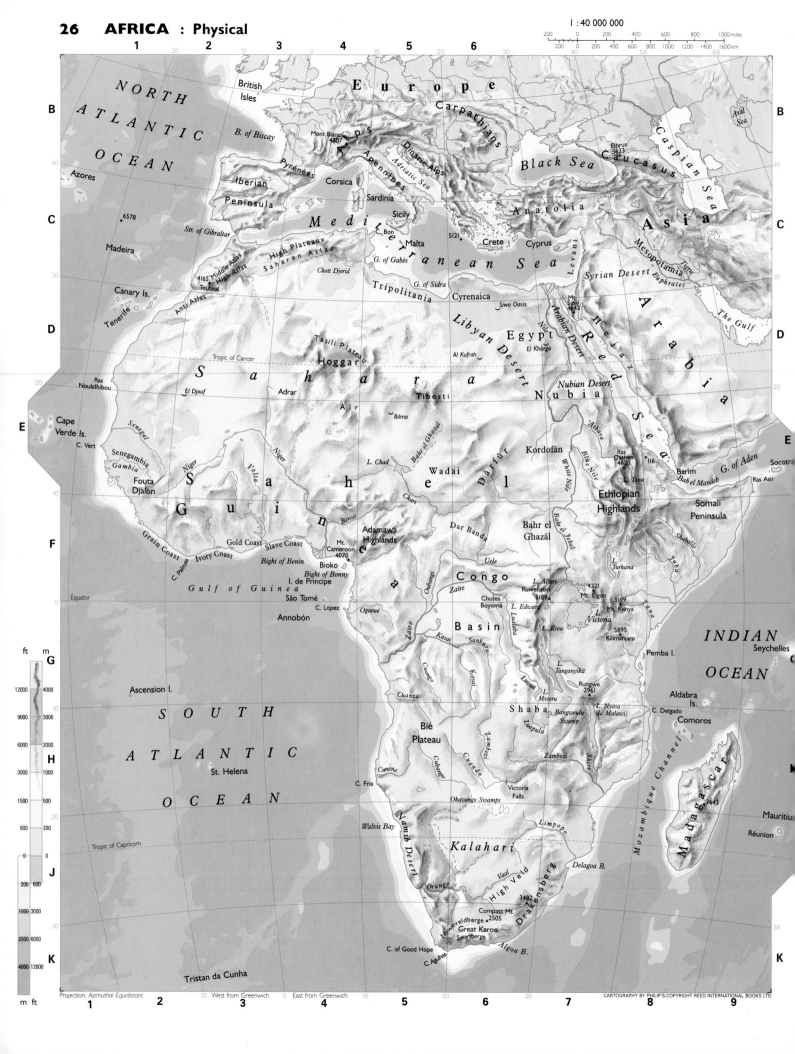

1 : 40 000 000

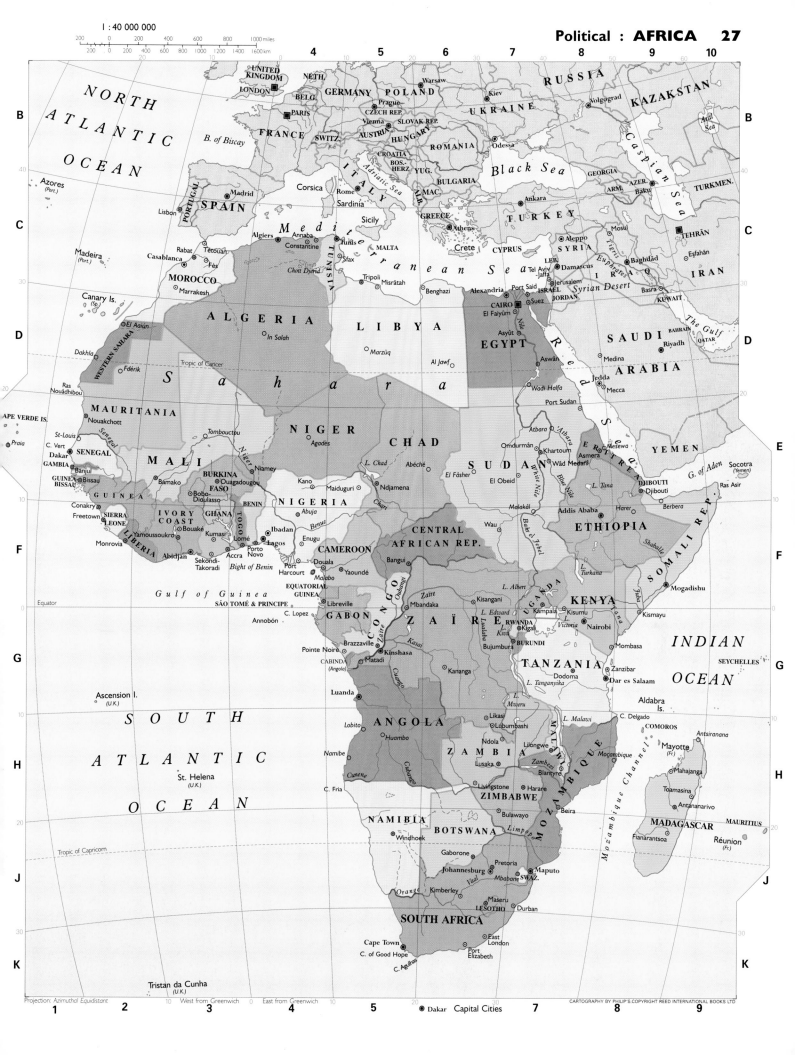

NORTH ATLANTIC

OCEAN

SPAIN

Cádiz · Málaga · Almería

Str. of Gibraltar
Gibraltar (U.K.)
Tangier · Ceuta (Sp.)
Tétouan · Al Hoceima · Melilla
Larache
Ksar el Kebir · Ouezzane · Oujda
Kenitra · Salé · Fès · Taza · Jerada
Rabat · Meknès
Casablanca · Berrechid · Khenifra
El Jadida · Settat · Khouribga
Safi · Beni Mellal
MOROCCO
Marrakesh · Ar Rachidya
Essaouira
Dj. Toubkal 4165
Agadir · Taroudannt
Anti Atlas
Ifni · Tiznit · Dra
Bou Izakarn
Mengoub

Oran · Mostaganem · Ech Cheliff · Algiers · Tizi-Ouzou · Bejaïa · Skikda · Annaba
Sidi-Bel-Abbès · Blida · Constantine · Guelma · Sétif
Tlemcen · Médéa · Batna · Khenchela
Saïda · Ksar el Boukhari · Biskra
Mecheria · El Bayadh · Djelfa · Laghouat · El Oued · Gabes
Aïn Sefra 2235 · Touggourt · Ghardaïa · Hassi Messaoud
Béchar · Beni Ounif · Ouargla
Abadla · Beni Abbès · Hassi er Rmel
Igli · Kerzaz
Ft. Mac-Mahon · Hassi Inifel · Ghudami
Ft. Miribel
Timimoun · Daraj
Charouine
Adrar · In Belbel · In Salah · Ohanet
Bj. Fly Ste. Marie · Miliana
Zaouiet Reggane · Aoulef el Arab · Bordj Omar Driss
Arak · Illizi
Ouallene · Bj.-Torat · Sardalas
Bj.-in-Eker · Idelès · Ghat · Djanet

ALGERIA

TUNISIA

Tindouf · Chegga

WESTERN SAHARA
Dakhla
C. Barbas
El Aaiún
Bu Craa
C. Bojador
Semara
Bir Mogrein
Aïn Ben Tili

MAURITANIA
Nouâdhibou · Ras Nouâdhibou · La Güera
Atâr · Ouadâne · Chinguetti
Oujeft
Fdérik · Zouérate · Châr
Terhazza
Taoudenni
Poste Maurice Cortier
Adrar des Iforhas
Tessalit · Admer

Hoggar · Tahat 2918 · Tamanrasset
Er Tanezrouft
El Djouf
Chech

MALI
Nouakchott
Boutilimit · Aleg · Tâmchekket
Mederdra · Kiffa · Akreijit · Tichît
Moudjéria · Togba
Rachid · Tidjikja
Akjoujt
Araouane
Bou Djébéha · Kidal
Mabrouk
Tombouctou · Bamba · Kerchoual
Goundam · Diré · Gourma-Rharous · Gao
Niafouke · Kabara
Bássikounou · Ansongo · Ménaka
Néma · Timbedgha
Ouâlâta
Kabara

NIGER
Aïr · Monts Tamgak
Iférouane · Agadez · Fachi
Audéras 1900
I-n-Gall
Tahoua · Tanout
Maské · Maradi · Zinder · Nguru
Madaoua · Tessaoua · Kamouguénam
Birni Nkonni · Gangara
Filingué · Gour. nel

SENEGAL
St. Louis · Dakar · Kaolack · Kaffrine
C. Vert · Thiès · Diourbel · Louga · Linguère · Matam
Tivaouane · Dahra
Rosso · Podor · Bogué · Kaédi
Dagana

GAMBIA
Banjul · Georgetown · Kolda · Tambacounda
Basse

GUINEA-BISSAU
Bissau · Bafatá · Gabú
Bolama · Zinguinchor

GUINEA
Conakry · Dubréka · Forécariah · Fouta Djalon
Boké · Télimélé · Pita · Dabola · Dinguiraye · Siguiri · Kankan
Kindia · Mamou · Faranah · Kissidougou · Kankan · Kouroussa
Boffa · Victoria · Dalaba · Kabala 1948

SIERRA LEONE
Freetown · Makeni · Magburaka · Koidu
Waterloo · Yonibana · Kenema
Bo · Sherbro I. · Bonthe

LIBERIA
Monrovia · Robertsport · Careysburg · Ganta
Marshall · Buchanan · Tapeta · Sanniquellie
River Cess · Greenville · Tai
Harper
C. Palmas · Tabou

IVORY COAST (CÔTE)
Abidjan · Grand Bassam · Assinie
Bouaké · Daloa · Yamoussoukro
Man · Danané · Guiglo · Gagnoa · Dimbokro
Odienné · Korhogo · Katiola · Bondoukou
Séguéla · Bouaflé
Sassandra · San-Pédro · Grand Lahou
C. Three Points

BURKINA FASO
Ouagadougou · Fada N'Gourma
Bobo-Dioulasso · Koudougou · Tenkodogo
Banfora · Léo
Djibo · Dori · Kaya · Diapaga

MALI
Bamako · Koulikoro · Ségou · Mopti · Douentza
Kita · Kati · Banamba · San · Djenné · Bandiagara · Hombori
Kayes · Kolokani · Sikasso · Koutiala · Bankass
Bafoulabé · Diafarabé · Ké-Macina · Sévaré
Nioro du Sahel · Nara · Niono · Sokolo
Sélibabi · Yélimané · Nara
Bakel · Satadougou · Kédougou · Kéniéba
Sarra

GHANA
Accra · Tema · Winneba · Cape Coast · Sekondi-Takoradi
Kumasi · Obuasi · Koforidua
Tamale · Yendi · Salaga
Wa · Bolgatanga · Navrongo
Sunyani · Techiman
Lake Volta · Ho · Kpandu

TOGO
Lomé · Aného · Atakpamé · Sokodé · Kara · Dapaong
Kpalimé · Blitta · Sokodé

BENIN
Porto-Novo · Cotonou · Abomey · Savé · Parakou · Kandi
Nikki · Djougou · Natitingou · Malanville

NIGERIA
Lagos · Ibadan · Abeokuta · Benin City · Onitsha · Enugu
Oyo · Ogbomosho · Oshogbo · Iwo · Ife · Ado-Ekiti · Owo · Ondo
Ilorin · Offa · Kabba · Lokoja · Makurdi · Wukari
Kaduna · Zaria · Kano · Katsina · Gusau · Sokoto
Bida · Minna · Jos · Bauchi · Gombe
Port Harcourt · Aba · Calabar · Okrika
Maiduguri · Potiskum · Azare

CAMEROON (CAMER)
Douala · Yaoundé · Mamfe · Bamenda
Mont Cameroun 4070 · Bioko · Rey Malabo · Kumba

Bight of Benin

1 : 8 000 000

50   0   50   100   150   200 miles
50   0   100   200   300 km

COPYRIGHT. GEORGE PHILIP LTD

CHAD

Lake Chad

N I G E R

M A L I

B U R K I N A   F A S O

UPPER

I V O R Y   C O A S T

G H A N A

NORTHERN

BRONG-AHAFO

ASHANTI

EASTERN

CENTRAL

WESTERN

ACCRA

Tema

Cape Coast

Sekondi-Takoradi

Kumasi

T O G O

B E N I N

Lomé

Cotonou

Porto-Novo

Abomey

N I G E R I A

BORNO

YOBE

JIGAWA

KANO

KATSINA

SOKOTO

KEBBI

NIGER

KADUNA

BAUCHI

PLATEAU

GONGOLA

ADAMAWA

TARABA

BENUE

KOGI

KWARA

OYO

OGUN

ONDO

EDO

DELTA

RIVER

CROSS

ABIA

ANAMBRA

IMO

LAGOS

IBADAN

Abeokuta

Ibadan

Ilorin

Ogbomosho

Oshogbo

Benin City

Warri

Port-Harcourt

Calabar

Aba

Onitsha

Enugu

Zaria

Kaduna

Kano

Maiduguri

Bauchi

Jos

Gombe

Yola

Makurdi

Abuja

FED. CAP. TERR.

C A M E R O O N

DOUALA

Yaoundé

Buea

Tiko

Edéa

BIOKO

EQUATORIAL GUINEA

G U L F   O F   G U I N E A

Bight of Benin

Niger Delta

Niger

East from Greenwich

Projection: Lambert's Equivalent Azimuthal

Niamey

Ouagadougou

Tombouctou (Timbuktu)

1 : 8 000 000

50   0   50   100   150   200 miles
50   0   100   200   300 km

COPYRIGHT GEORGE PHILIP & SON LTD.

Projection: Lambert's Equivalent Azimuthal

East from Greenwich

ZIMBABWE
MOZAMBIQUE
Maputo
SWAZILAND
BOTSWANA
NAMIBIA
LESOTHO

NORTHERN PROVINCE
NORTH WEST
GAUTENG
MPUMALANGA
FREE STATE
KWAZULU-NATAL
NORTHERN CAPE
EASTERN CAPE
WESTERN CAPE

SOUTH AFRICA

INDIAN OCEAN
ATLANTIC OCEAN

Kalahari
Namib Desert
Damaraland
Namaqualand
Great Karoo
Little Karoo
Drakensberg

Tropic of Capricorn

PRETORIA
JOHANNESBURG
Soweto
Germiston
Benoni
Springs
Vereeniging
Krugersdorp
Vanderbijlpark
Carletonville
Klerksdorp
Potchefstroom
Rustenburg
Brits
Pietersburg
Messina
Witbank
Middelburg
Nelspruit
Ermelo
Standerton
Bethal
Bloemfontein
Welkom
Virginia
Kroonstad
Kimberley
Bethlehem
Harrismith
Ladysmith
Newcastle
Vryheid
Dundee
Pietermaritzburg
DURBAN
Umlazi
KwaMashu
Empangeni
Richards Bay
Port Shepstone
Umtata
East London
King William's Town
Bisho
Grahamstown
PORT ELIZABETH
Uitenhage
Queenstown
Graaff-Reinet
Cradock
Middelburg
De Aar
Beaufort West
Oudtshoorn
George
Mossel Bai
Knysna
Swellendam
Worcester
Paarl
Stellenbosch
CAPE TOWN
Saldanha
Vredenburg
Moorreesburg
Upington
Springbok
Port Nolloth
Lüderitz
Keetmanshoop
Mariental
Windhoek
Walvis Bay
Swakopmund
Okahandja
Gobabis
Rehoboth
Bulawayo
Masvingo
Zvishavane
Gaborone
Mochudi
Kanye
Lobatse
Molepolole
Serowe
Palapye
Maun
Francistown
Plumtree
Maseru
C. of Good Hope
Table Mt. 1086
Agulhas

ERITREA

Dahlak Kebir I.
Mesewa
Asmera
Agordat
Kassala
Khashm el Girba
Gedaref
Khartoum
Omdurman
Wad Medani
Kosti
El Obeid
En Nahud
El Odaiya
El Fasher
El Geneina
Kutum

Mekele
Lalibela
Dese
Gonder
Debre Markos
ADDIS ABABA
ETHIOPIA
Jima
Nekemte
Gore
L. Tana
Ras Dashen 4620
Aksum
Dobra Tabor

L. Abaya
L. Shamo
Omo
Burji
Chew Bahir (L. Stefanie)
L. Turkana (L. Rudolf)

El Wak
Wajir
Marsabit
S. Horr
Moroto
Gulu

KENYA
Moyale 4321
Meru 5199
Nakuru
Eldoret
Kitale
Kisumu
Kericho
Thika
Machakos
Nairobi
Kilimanjaro 5895
Moshi
Arusha

Mombasa
& Kilindini
Tanga
Zanzibar
Pemba
Dar-es-Salaam
Mafia I.
Morogoro
Dodoma
Iringa
Njombe
Songea
Mtwara
C. Delgado
Lindi

TANZANIA
Mwanza
Musoma
L. Eyasi
Singida
Tabora
Nzega
Mbeya
L. Rukwa

L. Victoria
Kampala
Entebbe
Jinja
UGANDA
L. Kyoga
L. Albert
L. Edward
L. Kivu

RWANDA
Kigali
BURUNDI
Bujumbura
Bukavu
L. Tanganyika
Kigoma-Ujiji
Kalemie
Kabalo
Kongolo
Kindu
Kasongo
Kamina
Kananga
Luluabourg
Kolwezi
Likasi
Kabinda

ZAIRE
Kisangani
Bumba
Lisala
Mbandaka
Bandundu
Ilebo
Tshikapa
L. Mweru
Kananga

SUDAN
Wau
Juba
Malakal
Bor
Torit
Bahr el Jebel
White Nile
Sobat
Bahr el Arab

CHAD
Ndjamena
Abéché
Sarh
Moundou
Mongo
Ati
Bol
L. Chad
Bahr el Ghazal

CENTRAL AFRICAN REPUBLIC
Bangui
Bossangoa
Bouar
Berberati
Bambari
Bangassou

CAMEROON
Yaoundé
Douala
Maroua
Garoua
Ngaoundéré
Bamenda
Foumban
Bertoua
Ebolowa

NIGERIA
Kano
Maiduguri
Zinder
Jos
Makurdi
Lafia
Wukari
Azare
Bauchi

NIGER

EQUATORIAL GUINEA
Bata
Mbini
Libreville

GABON
Port Gentil
Lambaréné
Franceville
Oyem
C. St. Jean

CONGO
Brazzaville
Pointe Noire
Ouesso
Owando

KINSHASA
Matadi
Boma
Mbanza Ngungu
Kikwit
Kasongo-Lunda

CABINDA
Cabinda

ANGOLA
Luanda
Malanje
Ambriz
N'zeto

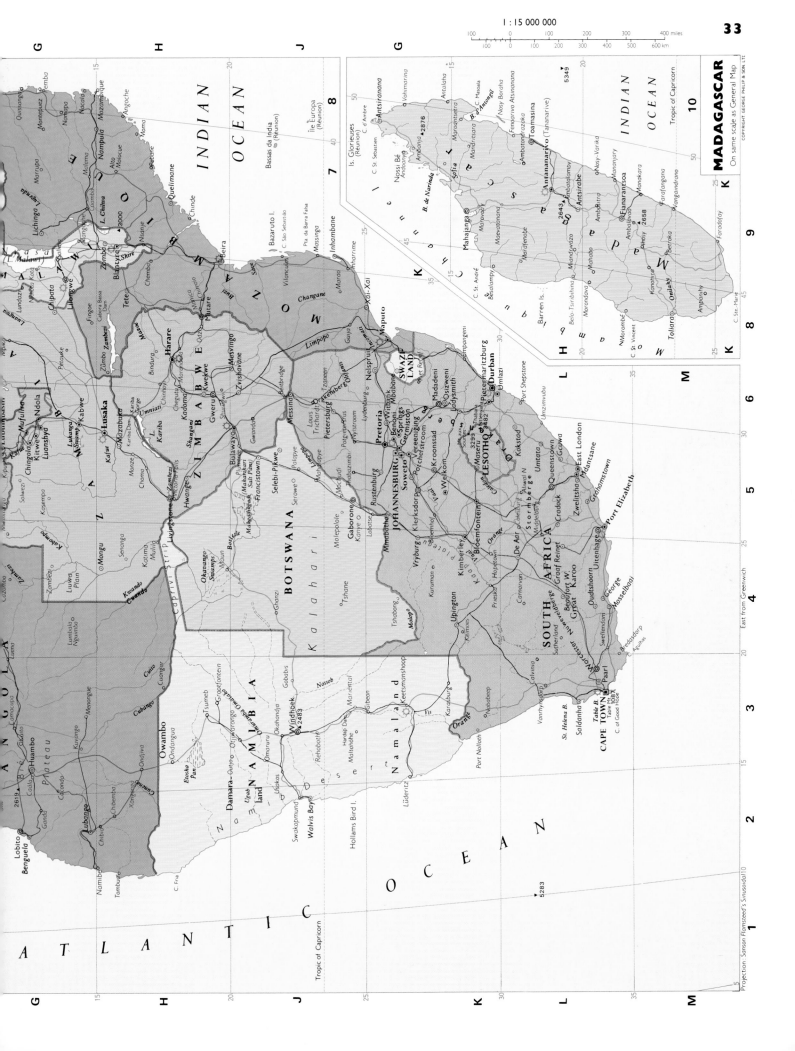

INDONESIA

Sulawesi (Celebes)
Kendari
5300
Butung
Ujung Pandang (Makasar)
Flores Sea
Sumbawa
Raba
Flores
Ende
Sumba
6204
Alor
Kupang
Timor
Dili
3310
Wetar
Leti
Babar
Timor Sea
Buru
Ambon
Ceram
Misool
Fakfak
Sorong
Vogelkop
Kai Is.
7260
3350
Aru Is.
Tanimbar Is.
Pulau Yos Sudarso
Irian Jaya
Jayapura
Pegunungan Maoke
Puncak Jaya 5020
Biak
Arafura Sea

New Guinea
PAPUA NEW GUINEA
Wewak
Madang
Mount Hagen
4508 Mt. Wilhelm
Lae
Fly
Gulf of Papua
Owen Stanley Range
Port Moresby
Torres Strait
Bismarck Archipelago
Kavieng
New Ireland
Rabaul
9140
New Britain
Solomon Sea
D'Entrecasteaux
Louisiade Archipelago

Coral Sea

C. York
Weipa
Cape York Peninsula
C. Croker
C. Arnhem
Melville I.
Darwin
Arnhem Land
Gulf of Carpentaria
Wellesley I.
Cooktown
Great Barrier Reef
Cairns
1611 Bartle Frere
Coral Sea Islands Territory

C. Londonderry
Cambridge G.
Wyndham
Derby
Broome
Kimberley Plateau
Larrimah
Daly Waters
Barkly Tableland
NORTHERN
TERRITORY
Tanami Desert
Tennant Creek
Mitchell
Normanton
Forsayth
Kajabbi
Filinders
Townsville
Charters Towers
Hughenden
Mount Isa
Great Sandy Desert
L. Mackay
Macdonnell Ranges
1510 Mt. Ziel
Alice Springs
Simpson Desert
QUEENSLAND
Winton
Longreach
Diamantina
Yaraka
Rockhampton
Gladstone
Bundaber
Maryborough
Gympie

N.W. Cape
Dampier
Port Hedland
Newman
Mt. Bruce 1226
Hamersley Range
Lake Disappointment
Gibson Desert
AUSTRALIA
WESTERN
L. Carnegie
Great Victoria Desert
AUSTRALIA
Ayers Rock
Mt. Woodroffe 1440
Musgrave Ranges
SOUTH
Lake Eyre
Cooper Creek
Grey Range
Charleville
Quilpie
Cunnamulla
Thargomindah
Roma
Toowoomba
BRISBAN
Ipswich
Gol
Coas
Lismor

Carnarvon
Murchison
Meekatharra
Leonora
AUSTRALIA
Marree
Warrego
Dirranbandi
Walgett
Bourke
Cobar
NEW SOUTH
Tamworth
Round Mt. 1615
Taree
Geraldton
Lake Barlee
Darling Range
Kalgoorlie-Boulder
Deakin
Tarcoola
Broken Hill
Flinders Range
Darling
Dubbo
WALES
Newcastle
Orange
Bathurst
SYDNEY
Wollongon
Shellharbour
Perth
Northam
Norseman
Nullarbor Plain
Penong
Port Augusta
Whyalla
Port Pirie
Murray
Mildura
Wagga Wagga
Mt. Kosciusko 2237
Canberra
CAPITAL TERRITORY
Bunbury
Esperance
Great Australian Bight
5632
Port Lincoln
Spencer Gulf
Adelaide
Encounter B.
Shepparton
Albury
Murray Australian Alps
Bombala
C. Howe
C. Leeuwin
Augusta
Albany
Kangaroo I.
Mount Gambier
Horsham
Bendigo
VICTORIA
Ballarat
MELBOURNE
Geelong
Warrnambool
King I.
Bass Strait
Furneaux Group
Burnie
Launceston
1617 Mt.Ossa
TASMANIA
Hobart
S.E. Cape

INDIAN OCEAN

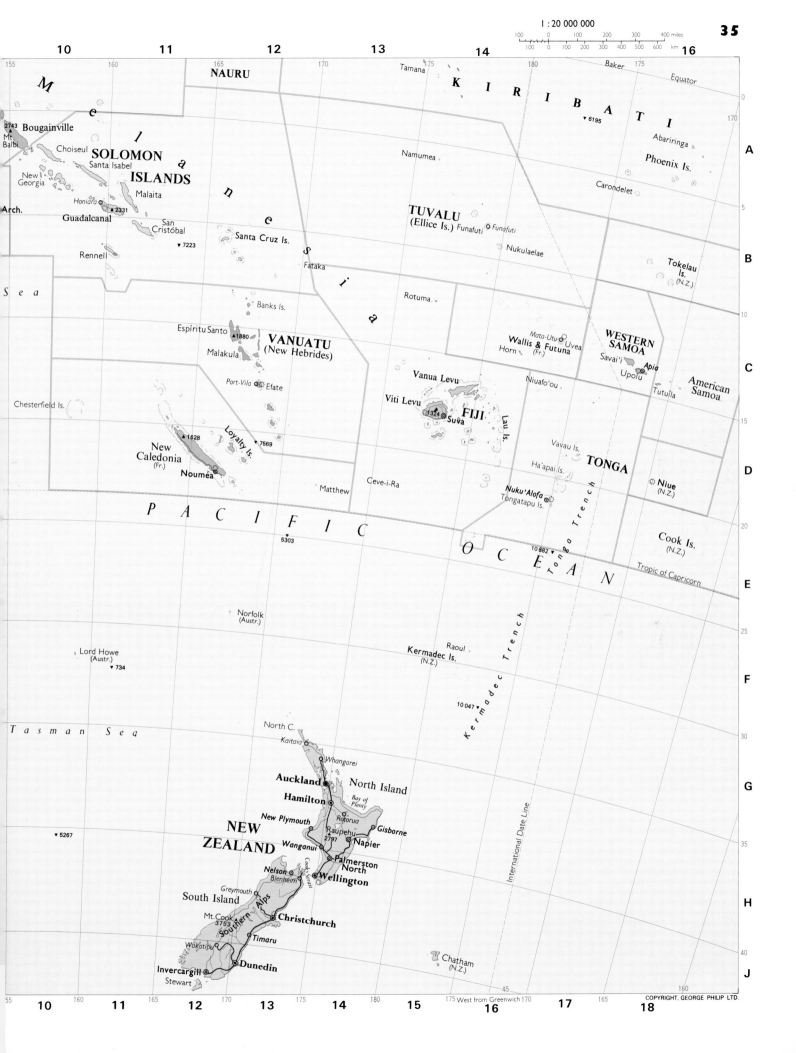

1 : 20 000 000

NAURU

M e l a n e s i a

K I R I B A T I

Tamana

Baker

Equator

▼6195

Abariringa

Bougainville
▲2743
Mt.
Balbi

Choiseul

SOLOMON
ISLANDS

Santa Isabel

Phoenix Is.

Namumea

Carondelet

New
Georgia

Malaita

Arch.

Honiara ⊙ ▲2331

Guadalcanal

San
Cristóbal

Rennell

Santa Cruz Is.

▼7223

TUVALU
(Ellice Is.) Funafuti ⊙ Funafuti

Nukulaelae

Tokelau
Is.
(N.Z.)

Sea

Fataka

Rotuma

WESTERN
SAMOA

Banks Is.

Espíritu Santo ▲1880

VANUATU
(New Hebrides)

Mata-Utu ⊙ Uvea
Wallis & Futuna
Horn   (Fr.)

Savai'i   Apia
Upolu

American
Samoa

Malakula

Vanua Levu

Niuafo'ou

Tutuila

Port-Vila ⊙ Efate

Viti Levu

Chesterfield Is.

Loyalty Is.

1324 ⊙
Suva

FIJI

Lau Is.

Vavau Is.

TONGA

New
Caledonia
(Fr.)

▲1628

▼7569

Ha'apai Is.

Nouméa ⊙

Matthew

Ceve-i-Ra

Niue
(N.Z.)

Nuku'Alofa ⊙
Tongatapu Is.

PACIFIC

Tonga Trench

▼5303

10 882 ▼

O C E A N

Tropic of Capricorn

Cook Is.
(N.Z.)

Norfolk
(Austr.)

Raoul

Lord Howe
(Austr.)
▼734

Kermadec Is.
(N.Z.)

Kermadec Trench

Tasman Sea

10 047 ▼

North C.

Kaitaia

▼5267

Whangarei

Auckland ⊙   North Island

Hamilton

Bay of
Plenty

New Plymouth

Rotorua

NEW
ZEALAND

Raupehu
2797

Gisborne

Wanganui

Napier

International Date Line

Palmerston
North

Nelson ⊙

Cook Strait

Wellington

Blenheim

Greymouth

South Island

Southern Alps

Christchurch

Mt.Cook
3759

Timaru

Wakatipu

Chatham
(N.Z.)

Invercargill ⊙ Dunedin

Stewart

West from Greenwich

Projection: Mollweide's Homolographic

11 12 13 14 15 16 17 18 19 20

A
B
C
D
E
F
G
H
J
K
L
M
N

North America

ALASKA
Bristol Bay
Gulf of Alaska
Prince of Wales I.
Queen Charlotte Is.
Kitimat
Prince Rupert
Juneau
6959
5959

GREENLAND
C. Farewell

NORTH

Hudson Bay
L. Winnipeg
Edmonton
Labrador
Newfoundland

C A N A D A

NORTH AMERICA

Vancouver
Vancouver I.
Victoria
Seattle
Portland
Calgary
Regina
Winnipeg
L. Superior
Montréal
Québec
Pr. Edward I.
Saint John
St. Lawrence
Minneapolis
L. Huron
L. Michigan
Ottawa
Toronto
L. Ontario
L. Erie
Detroit
Buffalo
Pittsburgh
Boston
C. Sable
NEW YORK
Philadelphia
Baltimore
Washington

CHICAGO

Cincinnati

ATLANTIC

C. Mendocino
Boise
Snake
Salt Lake City
Denver
Kansas
St. Louis
4418
Memphis
Atlanta
C. Hatteras

UNITED STATES

Oklahoma

San Francisco

Los Angeles
San Diego
Dallas
Jacksonville

Bermuda (U.K.)

OCEAN

Ciudad Juárez
San Antonio
Houston
New Orleans
Miami

6225
Monterrey
Gulf of Mexico
Havana
BAHAMAS
Florida Strait

Tropic of Cancer
Hawaiian Is. (U.S.)
Honolulu
Oahu
Hawaii

E X I C O
Sierra Madre
Gulf of California

Yucatan Channel
CUBA
West Indies
Hispaniola
DOM. REP.
9200

6741

Revilla Gigedo Is. (Mexico)
Guadalajara
Mérida
7680
HAITI
JAMAICA
Kingston
PUERTO RICO
Leeward Is.

M

Mexico
Puebla
5700
BELIZE
GUATEMALA
Guatemala
8862
HONDURAS
Caribbean Sea
BARBADOS
Windward Is.
TRINIDAD & TOBAGO

Acapulco
Salvador
EL SALVADOR
NICARAGUA
Managua
Barranquilla
Maracaibo
Caracas

Clipperton I. (Fr.)
CENTRAL AMERICA
COSTA RICA
San José
Colón
Panama
PANAMA
Canal
Orinoco
VENEZUELA

Cocos I.
Medellín
Bogotá
Cali
COLOMBIA

PACIFIC
N.W. Christmas Island Ridge
Palmyra Is. (U.S.)
Teraina
Tabuaeran
Kiritimati
Jarvis I. (U.S.)

Johnston I. (U.S.)
Laysan I.
Midway

Equator
Galápagos (Ecuador)
Guayaquil
Quito
ECUADOR
Iquitos
Manaus
Amazon

OCEAN
Sudbury I.
Phoenix Is.
KIRIBATI
Malden I.
Starbuck I.
C. Pariñas

BRAZIL

SOUTH

Tongareva
Penrhyn Is.
Manihiki
Vostok I.
Flint I.
Marquesas Is.
Caroline I.
Trujillo

Suwarrow Is.
Leeward Is.
Society Is.
Tahiti
Tuamotu Archipelago
PERU
Lima
6369

AMERICA

Cook Islands (N.Z.)
Windward Is.
Manuae
FRENCH POLYNESIA
Cuzco
L. Titicaca
Illampu & Ancohuma
6550

Rarotonga
Austral
Mururoa
6866
Peru-
Arequipa
La Paz
BOLIVIA

Tubuai Is. (Austral Is.)
Rapa Iti
Seamount Chain
Pitcairn I. (U.K.)
Ducie I. (U.K.)
Tropic of Capricorn
Iquique
Chile
8050
PARAGUAY
Antofagasta Trench
Asunción

Sala-y-Gomez (Chile)
Easter Is. (Chile)
San Félix (Chile)
San Ambrosio (Chile)
Tucumán

Pto. Alegre

Arch. de Juan Fernández (Chile)
Córdoba
6960
Rosario
URUGUAY
Valparaíso
Santiago
Buenos Aires
Montevideo
Río de la Plata

Chile Rise
Concepción
ARGENTINA

SOUTH

Chonos Arch.
Patagonia
ATLANTIC

G. of Penas
6212
OCEAN

East Pacific Ridge
Pacific-Antarctic Ridge

Punta Arenas
Str. of Magellan
Tierra del Fuego
C. Horn
Falkland Is. (U.K.)
South Georgia

West from Greenwich

11 12 13 14 15 16 17 18 19 20

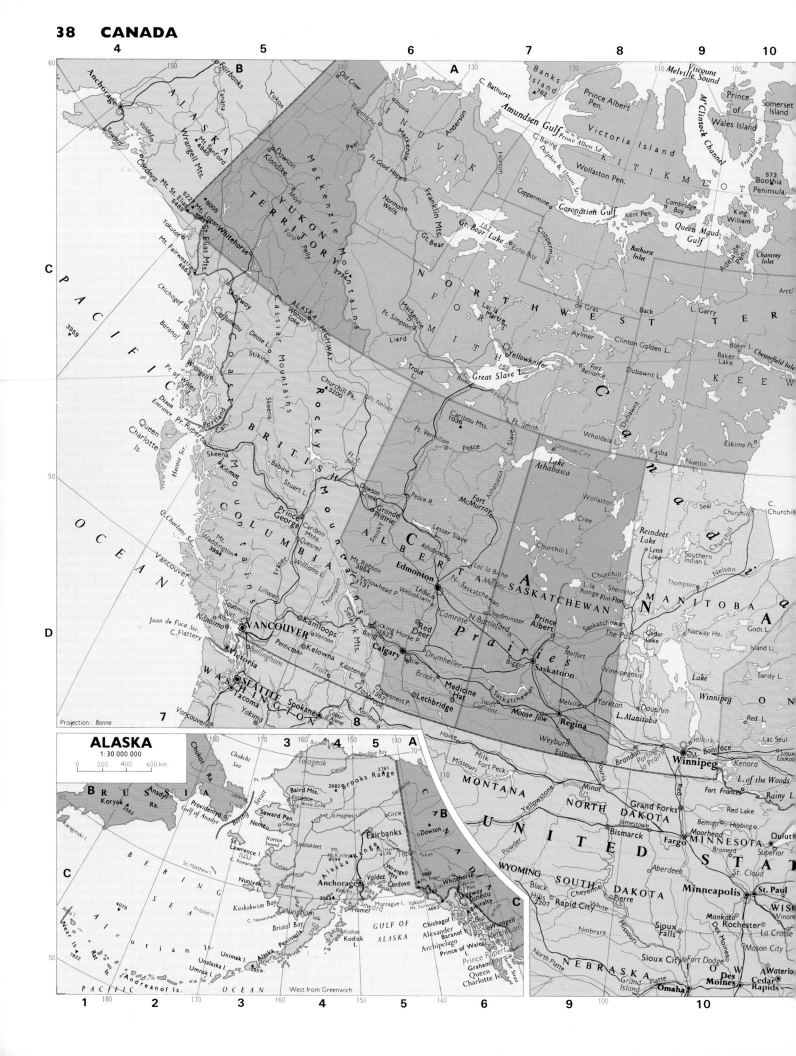

1 : 15 000 000

100   0   100   200   300   400 miles
100   0   100   200   300   400   500   600 km

11   12   13   14   15

Devon Island
Lancaster Sound
Brodeur
Peninsula
Bylot I.
2134
Pond Inlet
Baffin Bay
2136
Svartenhuk Peninsula
Disko I.
Sondre Stromfjord
G R E E N L A N D
Angmagssalik
King Frederick VI Coast
Godthåb
Frederikshaab
Julianehaab Sydprøven
C. Farewell

Foxe Basin
Prince Charles I.
Melville Peninsula
C. Hewett
Home B.
Cumberland Peninsula
2591
C. Mercy
Cumberland Sd.
C. Dyer
Davis Strait

A T L A N T I C

C. Dorchester
Foxe Channel
Nettilling L.
Amadjuak L.
Iqaluit
Frobisher Bay
Resolution I.
Foxe Penin.

Wager B.
Roes Welcome Sd.
Southampton I.
Coats I.
Mansel I.
Hudson Strait
Quaqtaq
Akpatok I.
C. Chidley

Chesterfield Inlet
King George Is.
Ivujivik
Kangiqsujuaq
Arnaud Kangirsuk
Ungava Bay
Kangiqsualujjuaq
1676
Naim
3809

H u d s o n
Ottawa Is.
258
Ungava Peninsula
Inukjuak
Feuilles
George R.
Hopedale
Indian Harbour
C. Harrison

B a y
King George Is.
Belcher Is.
C. Henrietta Maria
L. Minto
L. Bienville
Kuujjuarapik
Kaniapiskau
Scheffervile
Petitsikapau
Michikamau L.
Rigolet
Cartwright
Happy Valley
Goose Bay
Battle Harb.
Churchill

Severn
Winisk
Big Trout L.
Attawapiskat
Akimiski I.
James Bay
Chisasibi
Eastmain
Rupert
L.
Labrador City
1128
Gagnon
Str. of Belle Isle
Grand Falls
Gander
Bonavista
Carbonear
St. John's
C. Race

St. Joseph
Albany
Moosonee
Missinaibi
Waskaganish
Mistassini
Chibougamau
Manicouagan R.
Sept Iles
Port-Cartier
Anticosti
Mingan
Natashquan
Corner Brook
814
Channel Port aux Basques
Ray
Newfoundland

Thunder Bay
Geraldton
Nipigon
Oba
Hearst
Timmins
Kirkland Lake
Rouyn
Val d'Or
La Tuque
Gouin Reservoir
St. John
Saguenay
1190
Rivière du Loup
Edmundston
Bathurst
Chatham
NEW BRUNSWICK
Moncton
Amherst
New Glasgow
Sable I. (Nova Scotia)

Marquette
Sault Ste. Marie
Sudbury
North Bay
Ottawa R.
Cabonga Reservoir
Shawinigan
Trois Rivieres
Quebec
Thetford Mines
Sherbrooke
St. Hyacinthe
Fredericton
Saint John
Kentville
NOVA SCOTIA
Truro
Dartmouth
Bridgewater
Halifax

Thunder Bay
Escanaba
Lake Superior
Sault Ste. Marie
Georgian Bay
Peterboro
Ottawa
Hull
Cornwall
Kingston
Burlington
L. Champlain
MAINE
Bangor
6309
C. Sable
Yarmouth
B. of Fundy

Wausau
Green Bay
Appleton
MILWAUKEE
Madison
Traverse City
Owen Sound
Orillia
Oshawa
TORONTO
L. Ontario
Rochester
Syracuse
VERMONT
NEW HAMPSHIRE
Concord Manchester
Portland

Saginaw
London
Kitchener
Hamilton
Niagara Falls
St. Catharines
Lake Erie
BUFFALO
Albany
Springfield
MASS.
BOSTON
C. Cod
Providence

Grand Rapids
Rockford
Madison
DETROIT
Windsor
Sarnia
Erie
Binghamton
Scranton
NEW YORK
New Haven
CHICAGO
Gary
INDIANA
Toledo
OHIO
CLEVELAND
Akron
PENNSYLVANIA
Newark
NEW JERSEY
Allentown
ILLINOIS

C a n a d i a n   S h i e l d
O N T A R I O
Q U E B E C
L a b r a d o r
NEW YORK

11   12   13   14

BRITISH COLUMBIA

ALBERTA   SASKATCHEWAN   MANITOBA

WASHINGTON

OREGON

IDAHO

MONTANA

NORTH DAKOTA

SOUTH DAKOTA

WYOMING

NEVADA

UTAH

COLORADO

NEBRASKA

KANSAS

CALIFORNIA

ARIZONA

NEW MEXICO

OKLAHOMA

TEXAS

BAJA CALIFORNIA

BAJA CALIFORNIA SUR

SONORA

CHIHUAHUA

COAHUILA

DURANGO

MEXICO

PACIFIC OCEAN

Gulf of California

Great Basin

Coast Ranges

Rocky Mts.

Columbia Plateau

Colorado Plateau

Major cities and places

Vancouver, Victoria, New Westminster, Bellingham, Everett, Seattle, Tacoma, Olympia, Yakima, Spokane, Portland, Salem, Eugene, Bend, Medford, Klamath Falls, Vancouver, Richland, Walla Walla, Pendleton, Boise, Twin Falls, Idaho Falls, Pocatello, Winnemucca, Reno, Carson City, Elko, Sacramento, Santa Rosa, SAN FRANCISCO, Oakland, San Jose, Stockton, Fresno, Bakersfield, Santa Barbara, LOS ANGELES, Glendale, Long Beach, Anaheim, Santa Ana, Riverside, San Bernardino, San Diego, Tijuana, Mexicali, Ensenada, Las Vegas, Phoenix, Mesa, Tucson, Nogales, Yuma, Flagstaff, Gallup, Albuquerque, Santa Fe, Las Cruces, El Paso, Ciudad Juárez, Roswell, Carlsbad, Hobbs, Midland, Odessa, San Angelo, Lubbock, Amarillo, Lawton, Wichita Falls, Abilene, Fort Worth, Salt Lake City, Ogden, Provo, Logan, Rock Springs, Denver, Colorado Springs, Pueblo, Greeley, Fort Collins, Cheyenne, Laramie, Casper, Scottsbluff, North Platte, Grand Island, Garden City, Hutchinson, Calgary, Lethbridge, Medicine Hat, Swift Current, Moose Jaw, Regina, Saskatoon, Brandon, Billings, Great Falls, Missoula, Helena, Butte, Havre, Bismarck, Jamestown, Aberdeen, Pierre, Rapid City, Mitchell, Hermosillo, Guaymas, Ciudad Obregón, Los Mochis, Chihuahua, Piedras Negras, Nuevo Laredo, Laredo, Monclova, Monterrey, Torreón, Gómez Palacio, Eagle Pass, Del Rio, San Antonio, Matamoros

Mountains and peaks

Mt. Rainier 4392, Mt. Hood 3427, Mt. Shasta 4317, Lassen Pk. 3187, Mt. Whitney 4418, Wheeler Pk. 3982, Grand Teton 4196, Gannett Pk. 4202, Humphreys Pk. 3851, Mt. Taylor 3445, Baldy Pk. 3476, Santa Blanca 3659, Roof Butte 2989, Blanca Pk. 4378, Mt. Elbert 4399, Black Hills 2207, Mt. Assiniboine 3618, Hyndman Pk. 3681

Water features

Lake Winnipegosis, L. Manitoba, Lake Oahe, Lake Sakakawea, Fort Peck L., Yellowstone, Great Salt Lake 1282, Utah L., Bear L., Pyramid L., Walker L., Lake Tahoe, Mono L., Lake Mead, Lake Powell, Salton Sea, Franklin D. Roosevelt L., Pend Oreille L., Kootenay Lake, Upper Arrow Lake, Lower Arrow Lake, Goose L., Summer L., Harney L., Malheur L., Upper Klamath L., Carson Sink

Rivers

Columbia, Snake, Missouri, Milk, Yellowstone, Bighorn, Wind River, Green, Colorado, Arkansas, North Platte, South Platte, Republican, Platte, Rio Grande, Pecos, Canadian, North Canadian, Cimarron, Red, Brazos, Llano Estacado, Gila, Sacramento, San Joaquin, Humboldt, Sevier, Verde, Gunnison, Niobrara, Smoky Hill, Salado, Conchos, Yaqui, Fuerte

Zion Nat. Park, Grand Canyon Nat. Park, Yosemite National Park, Sequoia Nat. Park, Yellowstone National Park, Glacier Nat. Park, Grand Canyon, Death Valley -86, Painted Desert, Mojave Desert, Sonora Desert, Bad Lands, Sand Hills, Smoky Hills

Selkirk Mts., Lewis Ra., Bitterroot Range, Salmon River Mts., Absaroka Range, Bighorn Mts., Wind River Ra., Uinta Mts., Wasatch, Front Range, Park Range, Sangre de Cristo Mts., San Juan Mts., White Mts., Sierra Nevada, Coast Ranges, Santa Lucia Ra., Tehachapi Pass, Sierra Madre, S. Andres Mts., Sacramento Mts., Black Ra., Laramie Mts., Plateau

Projection: Albers' Equal Area with two standard parallels
West from Greenwich

HAWAII
1 : 10 000 000

PACIFIC OCEAN

Kauai, Niihau, Oahu, Honolulu, Molokai, Lanai, Maui, Lahaina, Hilo, Hawaiian Islands

Kauai Channel, Kaiwi Channel, Kalohi Channel, Alenuihaha Channel, Kilauea Crater, Haleakala 3055, Mauna Kea 4205, Mauna Loa 4169

Kilauea Crater

20   40   60   80 miles
20 0 40 80 120 km

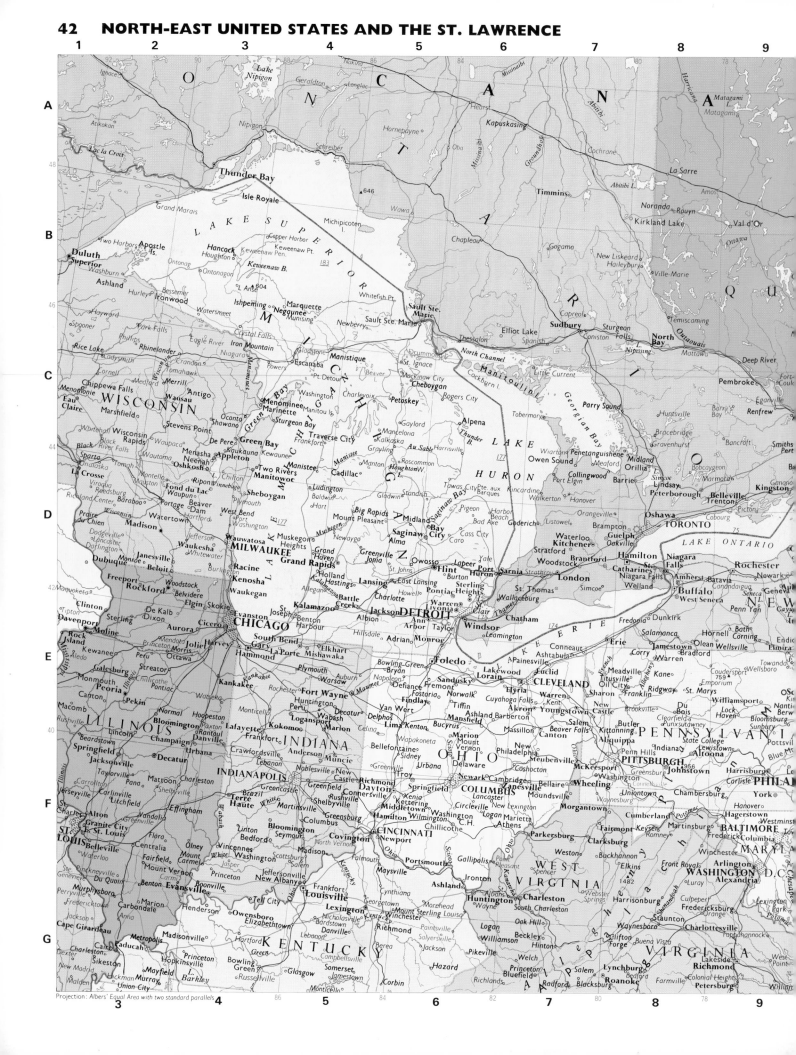

Projection: Albers' Equal Area with two standard parallels

10   11   12   13   14

A

D   556▲   Chibougamau   Chibougamau L.   Pipmuacan L.   A   West Pt.   *Anticosti I.*   60

Jupiter   62   Heath Pt.

St. Félicien   Cap-Chat   1310▲   C. Gaspé   ▼572

Gouin   Dolbeau   Lac   Matane   Shickshock Mts.   C. Gaspé   GULF OF   48

Res.   St. Jean   Gaspé Peninsula   ST. LAWRENCE

Roberval   Chicoutimi   Rimouski

É   Jonquière   Saguenay   Magdalen   C. North   B

Rivière du Loup   Campbellton   Dalhousie   *Chaleur Bay*   Is.

B   La Tuque   Baie St. Paul   Edmundston   819▲   N E W   Bathurst   (Quebec)   532▲   Cape Breton

E   C   Res.   Fort   Van   Grand   Newcastle   Chatham   Miramichi B.   North Pt.   PRINCE EDWARD   Island

Baskatong   Kent   Buren   Falls   B R U N S W I C K   Tignish   ISLAND   Glace Bay

Grand-Mère   Île d'Orléans   Eagle   Caribou   Summerside   East Pt.   Sydney

Shawinigan   Quebec   Louzon   Lake   Presque Isle   St. John   Charlottetown   Bras d'Or

L'Annonciation   968▲   Cap-de-la-Madeleine   Lévis   Eagle L.   Chamberlain   Moncton   Chédabucto B.

Trois-Rivières   Ste-Marie   Chesuncook   L.   Houlton   Fredericton   Grand L.   New Glasgow

L'Annonciation   Louiseville   Plessisville   St-George   1606▲   Patten   Springhill   Stellarton   Canso

Joliette   Victoriaville   Thetford   L.   Moosehead   Chiputneticook   Sussex   Truro   N O V A   C

St-   Sorel   Mines   Lac-   L.   Millinocket   Lakes   Saint   Kentville

Jérôme   Drummondville   Asbestos   Mégantic   Greenville   Mattawamkeug   John   Bay of Fundy   Dartmouth

Hawkesbury   St-   MONTREAL   St-Hyacinthe   Dover   Lincoln   St. Stephen   Digby   S C O T I A   Halifax

uckingham   Ottawa   Lachine   Granby   Sherbrooke   Foxcroft   Galais   East-port   Bridgewater

rior   St-Jean   Magog   M A I N E   Old Town   Grand   44

Hull   Cornwall   Beauharnois   Coaticook   Richardson   Brewer   Machias   Manan I.

arleton   Malone   Newport   Cowansville   Lakes   Bangor   Rossignol Res.   C. Sable

Place   Massena   Plattsburg   St. Albans   Island Pond   Rangeley   Skowhegan   Ellsworth   D

Prescott   Ogdensburg   Potsdam   Champlain   Winooski   St   Farmington   Waterville   Bur   Yarmouth

kville   Canton   Burlington   Johnsbury   Berlin   Rumford   Belfast   Harbor

Saranac Lakes   1629▲   Montpelier   Lancaster   Mt.   Augusta   Mt. Desert

Watertown   Gouverneur   V E R M O N T   Barre   Washington   Gardiner   Penobscot B.

Lowville   Adirondack Mts   Middlebury   White   1917   Lewiston   Rockland

ego   Lake Pleasant   Ticonderoga   Mts.   Conway   Auburn   Bath

lton   Rome   L. George   Rutland   Lebanon   Brunswick   D

Oneida   Claremont   Granville   Westbrook   Portland

neida   Utica   Glens   Hudson   Springfield   Franklin   Saco

Syracuse   Gloversville   Falls   Saratoga Springs   Concord   Dover   Biddeford

York   Schenectady   Amsterdam   Brattleboro   Keene   Manchester   Rochester

Cortland   Norwich   Troy   Greenfield   N   Nashua   Haverhill   Portsmouth

Albany   Fitchburg   Lowell   Newburyport   42

Oneonta   Pittsfield   Leominster   Lawrence   C. Ann

Binghamton   Catskill   Northampton   Worcester   Salem

City   Catskill Mts   1281▲   Chicopee   Cambridge   BOSTON

Springfield   M A S S .   Quincy   Cape Cod   E

Kingston   Hartford   Woonsocket   Brockton

Carbondale   Poughkeepsie   New Britain   Pawtucket   Taunton

Dunmore   Newburgh   Waterbury   Providence   Fall River

Wilkes   Middletown   Beacon   Meriden   C O N N .   R . I .   Warwick   New   Bedford

Barre   Danbury   New-   Newport   Martha's

Hazelton   Bridgeport   Haven   New   Vineyard

henandoah   Paterson   Stamford   London   Block I.   Nantucket

Easton   Yonkers   Mount   Long Island   Riverhead   40

Bethlehem   Jersey City   Vernon   Long Island

lentown   Newark   NEW YORK

Reading   Elizabeth   New Brunswick

ELPHIA   Pottstown   Trenton   Long Branch

ncaster   Norristown   Asbury Park   F

Camden   N E W

Chester   J E R S E Y

Wilmington   Hammonton

ewark   Bridgeton   Vineland

Milford   Millville   Atlantic City

ND   Dover   Ocean City   A T L A N T I C

polis   Cape May

Milford   Henlopen   38

Cambridge   D E L A W A R E   Seaford   O C E A N

Salisbury

Snow Hill   G

Accomac

76   10   74   West from Greenwich   72   11   12   70   13   68   14   66   15   64   16

C. Charles

rg   Charles

Bay

A   B   C   D

Roath A-1

CARIBBEAN SEA

ATLANTIC OCEAN

Equator

LESSER ANTILLES
Windward Is.
Martinique (Fr.)
ST. LUCIA
ST. VINCENT
THE GRENADINES
BARBADOS
GRENADA
Tobago
TRINIDAD & TOBAGO
P. of Spain

Margarita
Curaçao
Aruba (Neth.)
Bonaire
NETH. ANTILLES

Pta. Gallinas
Sta. Marta
Barranquilla
Cartagena
Ciénaga
5800
G. de Venezuela
Maracaibo
L. de Maracaibo
Cabimas
Trujillo
Mérida
Cord. de Mérida 5007
S. Cristóbal
Cúcuta
Bucaramanga
Barrancabermeja

PANAMA
Panamá
G. de Panamá
Darién
G. of Darién
Quibdó
C. Corrientes
Buenaventura
Pta. Galera
Esmeraldas

COLOMBIA
BOGOTÁ
Tunja
Villavicencio
San Gil
Meta
Medellín
Manizales
Ibagué
Palmira
Cali
Popayán
Pasto
Neiva
5750
Florencia
Mocoa
Putumayo
Macoa

ECUADOR
Quito
Cotopaxi 5897
Latacunga
Ambato
Chimborazo 6267
Riobamba
Cuenca
Macháta
Loja
Guayaquil
G. de Guayaquil
Pta. Parinas

VENEZUELA
CARACAS
Maiquetía
La Guaira
Barcelona
Cumaná
Maturín
Valencia
Barquisimeto
Puerto Felipe
Puerto Cabello
Ciudad Guayana
Ciudad Bolívar
Orinoco
Caicara
Pto. Carreño
Guaviare
Vichada

Tucupita
Cuyuni
El Callao
Angel Falls
Roraima 2810
Sa. Pacaraima
RORAIMA
Boa Vista
Branco

GUYANA
Georgetown
New Amsterdam
SURINAM
Paramaribo
Juliantop 1280
FR. GUIANA
Cayenne
C. Orange
Oyapoque
Islands
Highlands
Guiana

PERU
LIMA
Callao
Cerro de Pasco
Huánuco
Huancayo
Huancavelica
Ayacucho
Cuzco
N. Ausangate 6384
Abancay
Arequipa
Mollendo
Cajamarca
Chiclayo
Pimentel
Pacasmayo
Trujillo
Chimbote
Huaraz
Huascarán 6768
Yerupajá 6632
Piura
Iquitos
Yurimaguas
Chachapoyas
Marañón
Huallaga
Ucayali
Napo
Pastaza

AMAZONAS
Manaus
Negro
Madeira
Purus
Juruá
Javari
Içá
Japurá
Solimões
Caquetá
Putumayo
Tapajós
Trombetas
Amazon
Benjamin Constant

BRAZIL
AMAPÁ
Macapá
Amapá
I. de Marajó
B. de Marajó
Belém (Pará)
Santarém
Xingu
Tapajós
PARÁ
MARANHÃO
São Luís
Imperatriz
Bacabal
Caxias
B. de São Marcos
B. de São José
Parnaíba
Teresina
Sobral
Fortaleza
Camocim
Mossoró
Macau
C. de São Roque
Natal
RIO GRANDE DO NORTE
João Pessoa
Campina Grande
PARAÍBA
Recife
PERNAMBUCO
ALAGOAS
Maceió
SERGIPE
Aracaju
SALVADOR
B. de Todos os Santos
Ilhéus
CEARÁ
PIAUÍ
Juazeiro do Norte
Paulistana
Juàzeiro
Sobradinho Reservoir
S. Francisco
S. Senhor do Bonfim
Feira de Santana
BAHIA
Vitória da Conquista
Montes Claros
Teófilo Otoni
Gov. Valadares 2890
ESPÍRITO SANTO
Vitória
MINAS GERAIS
BELO HORIZONTE
Brasília
GOIÁS
Goiânia
Uberlândia
Uberaba
Ribeirão Preto
São José do Rio Preto
SÃO PAULO
Luz de Fora
TOCANTINS
Tocantins
Araguaia
Marabá
Capeiras Falls
Caxias
MATO GROSSO
Plateau of Mato Grosso
Cuiabá
MATO GROSSO DO SUL
Campo Grande
RONDÔNIA
Pto. Velho
Guaporé
ACRE
Rio Branco
Abunã

BOLIVIA
LA PAZ
Illimani 6550
Illampu 6550
Ancohuma
L. Titicaca
Cochabamba
Santa Cruz
Oruro
L. de Poopó
Potosí
Sucre
Trinidad
Mamoré
Beni
Madre de Dios
Puerto Maldonado
Sajama 6520
Salar de Uyuni
Tarija
Arica
Tacna
Iquique
Mollendo
Pto. Coca

Equator

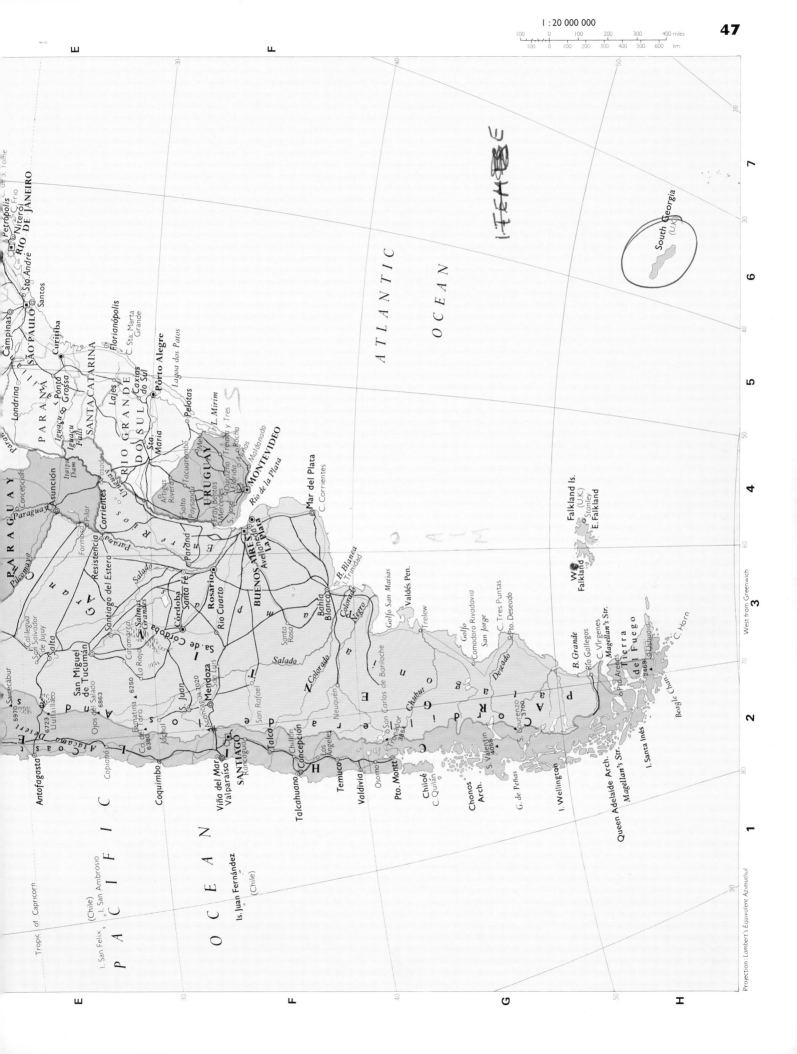

1 : 20 000 000

100   0   100   200   300   400 miles
100   0   100 200 300 400 500 600 km

ITEM 3E

ATLANTIC

OCEAN

South Georgia (U.K.)

C. São Tomé
C. Frio
Petrópolis
Niterói
RIO DE JANEIRO
Sto. André
São Paulo
Santos
Campinas

Londrina
SÃO PAULO
Curitiba
PARANÁ
Ponta Grossa
Iguaçu
Iguaçu Falls
Itaipú Dam
Florianópolis
SANTA CATARINA
C. Sta. Marta Grande
Lajes
Caxias do Sul
RIO GRANDE DO SUL
Porto Alegre
Lagoa dos Patos
Pelotas
Sta. Maria
L. Mirim

PARAGUAY
Asunción
Concepción
Paraguay
Pilar
Formosa
Resistencia
Corrientes
Posadas
Artigas
Uruguay
Salto
Paysandú
Rivera
Tacuarembó
Bento Gonçalves
Mercedes
Fray Bentos
S. José
Melo
Treinta y Tres
Rocha
Durazno
Florida
Minas
Maldonado
MONTEVIDEO
URUGUAY
Río de la Plata

Salta
San Salvador de Jujuy
Callegua
Calilegua
Antofagasta
Salinas Grandes
Catamarca
Santiago del Estero
La Rioja
S. de Córdoba
Córdoba
Río Cuarto
Santa Fé
Rosario
Paraná
BUENOS AIRES
La Plata
Avellaneda
Mar del Plata
C. Corrientes

GRAN
CHACO
PAMPA
Salado
Salado
Santa Rosa
Colorado
Río Colorado
Negro
B. Blanca
Bahía Blanca
I. Trinidad

Copiapó
Co. del Toro 6380
Fagatina 6250
Ojos del Salado 6863
San Juan
Júchal
San Luis
San Rafael
Mendoza
Aconcagua 7020
Santiago
Viña del Mar
Valparaíso
Rancagua
Talca
Chillán
Concepción
Los Ángeles
Talcahuano
Temuco
Valdivia
Osorno
Pto. Montt
Chiloé
C. Quilán
Chonos Arch.
G. de Peñas
I. Wellington
Queen Adelaide Arch.
Magellan's Str.
I. Santa Inés

Neuquén
San Carlos de Bariloche
Tronador 3854
S. Valentín 4058
S. Lorenzo 3700

Golfo San Matías
Valdés Pen.
Trelew
Chubut
Golfo San Jorge
Comodoro Rivadavia
C. Tres Puntas
Pto. Deseado
Deseado
Río Gallegos
B. Grande
C. Vírgenes
Magellan's Str.
Pta. Arenas
Tierra del Fuego 2469
Ushuaia
Beagle Chan.
C. Horn

Salmas
Grandes

PATAGONIA

ANDES

CORDILLERA

Falkland Is. (U.K.)
Stanley
W. Falkland
E. Falkland

PACIFIC
OCEAN

Antofagasta
Socaire
Socompa
Llullaillaco
Salar de Atacama
Atacama Desert
Tropic of Capricorn
I. San Félix (Chile)
I. San Ambrosio (Chile)
Coquimbo
Is. Juan Fernández (Chile)

Tropic of Capricorn

West from Greenwich

Projection Lambert's Equivalent Azimuthal

Paraná
Pilcomayo
Bermejo
Salado

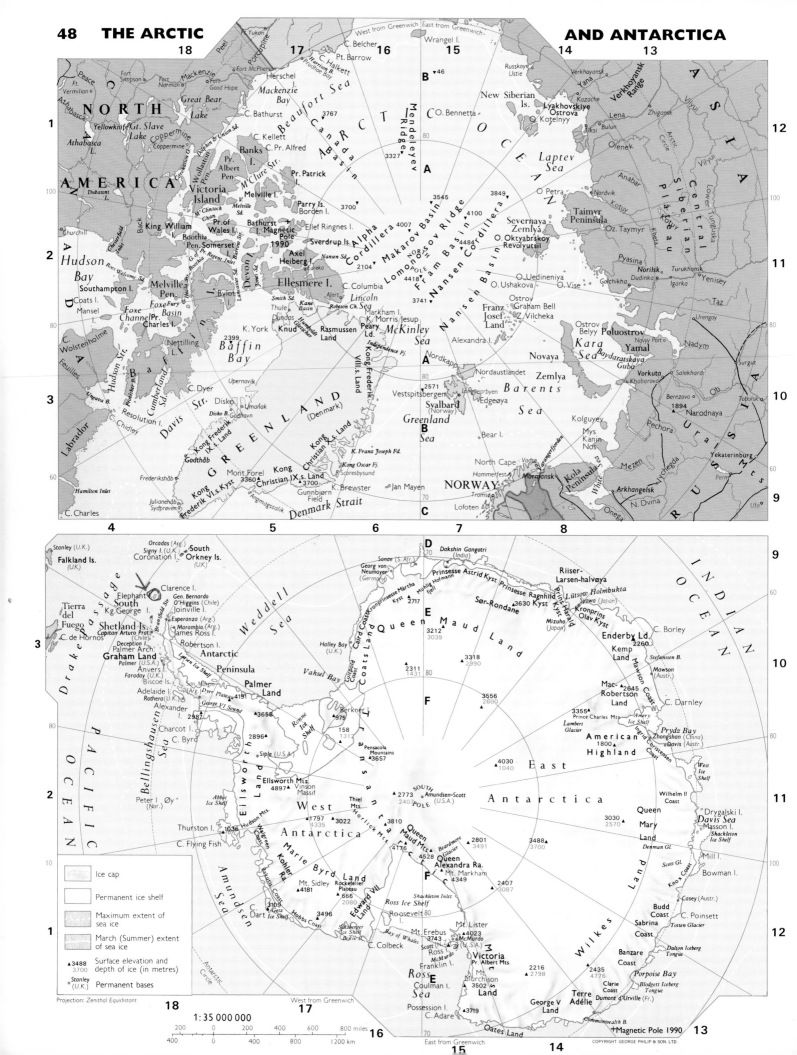

INDEX

The index contains the names of all the principal places and features shown on the maps. The alphabetical order of names composed of two or more words is governed primarily by the first word and then by the second. This is an example of the rule:

New South Wales □ **34** G8
New York □ **43** D9
New York City **43** E11
New Zealand ■ **35** J13
Newark, Del., U.S.A. **43** F10

Physical features composed of a proper name (Erie) and a description (Lake) are positioned alphabetically by the proper name. The description is positioned after the proper name and is usually abbreviated:

Erie, L. **42** D7

Where a description forms part of a settlement or administrative name, however, it is always written in full and put in its true alphabetical position:

Mount Isa **34** E6

Names beginning with M' and Mc are indexed as if they were spelt Mac. Names beginning St. are alphabetized under Saint, but Santa and San are all spelt in full and are alphabetized accordingly. If the same placename occurs two or more times in the index and all are in the same country, each is followed by the name of the administrative subdivision in which it is located. The names are placed in the alphabetical order of the subdivision. For example:

Columbus, Ga., U.S.A. **41** D10
Columbus, Ind., U.S.A. **42** F5
Columbus, Ohio, U.S.A. **42** F6

The number in bold type which follows each name in the index refers to the number of the map page where that feature or place will be found. This is usually the largest scale at which the place or feature appears.

The letter and figure which are in lighter type immediately after the page number give the grid square on the map page, within which the feature is situated. The letter represents the latitude and the figure the longitude. In some cases the feature itself may fall within the specified square, while the name is outside.

Rivers are indexed to their mouths or confluences, and carry the symbol → after their names. A solid square ■ follows the name of a country, while an open square □ refers to a first order administrative area.

Aachen **10** C4
Aalborg **6** G9
Aarau **10** E5
Aare → **10** E5
Aarhus **6** G10
Abadan **24** B3
Abbeville **8** A4
Abéché **29** F9
Abeokuta **30** C2
Aberdeen **7** C5
Abidjan **28** G4
Abitibi L. **42** A8
Abkhazia □ **15** F7
Abohar **23** D5
Abu Dhabi **24** C4
Abuja **30** C3
Acapulco **44** D5
Accomac **43** G10
Accra **30** C1
Acklins I. **45** C10
Aconcagua **47** F3
Acre □ **46** C2
Adamawa Highlands **29** G7
Adana **15** G6
Adapazarı **15** F5
Addis Ababa **29** G12
Adelaide, Australia **34** G6
Adelaide, S. Africa **31** C4
Aden **24** D3
Aden, G. of **24** D3
Adirondack Mts. **43** D10
Admiralty Is. **36** H6
Ado-Ekiti **30** C3
Adoni **25** D6
Adour → **8** E3
Adrar **28** C4
Adrian **42** E5
Adriatic Sea **12** C6
Ægean Sea **13** E11
Afghanistan ■ **24** B5
'Afif **24** C3
Agadès **30** A3
Agadir **28** B3
Agartala **23** H13
Agen **8** D4
Agra **23** F6
Agrigento **12** F5
Aguascalientes **44** C4
Agulhas, C. **31** C3
Ahmadabad **23** H4
Ahmadnagar **25** D6
Ahmadpur **23** E3
Ahvaz **24** B3
Ahvenanmaa Is. **6** F11
Aïr **28** E6
Aisne → **8** B5
Aix-en-Provence **8** E6
Aix-les-Bains **8** D6
Ajaccio **8** F8
Ajanta Ra. **23** J5
Ajaria □ **15** F7
Ajmer **23** F5
Akashi **19** B4
Akita **19** A7
Akola **23** J6
Akranes **6** B2
Akron **42** E7
Aktyubinsk **15** D10
Akure **30** C3
Akureyri **6** B4
Al Ḥudaydah **24** D3
Al Hufūf **24** C3
Al Jawf **24** C2
Al Kut **24** B3
Al Qatif **24** C3
Al 'Ula **24** C2
Alabama □ **41** D9
Aland Is. = Ahvenanmaa Is. **6** F11
Alaska □ **38** B5
Alaska, G. of **38** C5
Alaska Peninsula **38** C4
Alaska Range **38** B4
Alba-Iulia **11** E12
Albacete **9** C5
Albania ■ **13** D9
Albany, Australia **34** H2
Albany, Ga., U.S.A. **41** D10
Albany, N.Y., U.S.A. **43** D11
Albany → **39** C11
Albert L. **32** D6
Alberta □ **38** C8
Albertville **8** D7
Albi **8** E5
Albion **42** D5
Albuquerque **40** C5
Albury **34** H8
Alcalá de Henares **9** B4
Aldabra Is. **27** G8
Aldan → **18** C14
Aleksandrovsk-Sakhalinskiy **18** D16
Alençon **8** B4
Alès **8** D6
Alessándria **12** B3
Ålesund **6** F9
Aleutian Is. **36** B10
Alexander Arch. **38** C6
Alexandria, Egypt **29** B10
Alexandria, La., U.S.A. **41** D8
Alexandria, Va., U.S.A. **42** F9
Algarve **9** D1
Algeciras **9** D3
Algeria ■ **28** C5
Algiers **28** A5
Alicante **9** C5
Alice Springs **34** E5
Aligarh **23** F7
Alipur Duar **23** F12
Aliquippa **42** E7
Aliwal North **31** C4
Alkmaar **10** B3
Allahabad **23** G8
Allegan **42** D5
Allegheny → **42** E8
Allegheny Plateau **42** G7
Allentown **43** E10
Alleppey **25** E6
Allier → **8** C5
Alma **42** D5
Almaty **18** E9
Almelo **10** B4
Almería **9** D4
Alor **22** D4
Alpena **42** C6
Alps **10** E5
Alsace **8** B7
Altai **20** B4
Altay **20** B3
Altoona **42** E8
Altun Shan **20** C3
Alwar **23** F6
Amadjuak L. **39** B12
Amagasaki **19** B4
Amarillo **40** C6
Amazon → **46** C4
Ambala **23** D6
Ambikapur **23** H9
Ambon **22** D4
American Samoa ■ **35** C17
Amiens **8** B5
Amman **24** B2
Amos **42** A8
Amravati **23** J6
Amreli **23** J3
Amritsar **23** D5
Amroha **23** E7
Amsterdam, Neths. **10** B3
Amsterdam, U.S.A. **43** D10
Amudarya → **18** E7
Amundsen Gulf **38** A7
Amundsen Sea **48** E1
Amur → **18** D16
An Najaf **24** B3
An Nasiriyah **24** B3
An Nhon **22** B2
Anadyr **18** C19
Anadyr, G. of **18** C20
Anaheim **40** D3
Anambas Is. **22** C2
Anantnag **23** C5
Anar **24** B4
Anatolia **15** G5
Anchorage **38** B5
Ancona **12** C5
Anda **21** B7
Andalucía □ **9** D3
Andaman Is. **25** D8
Anderson **42** E5
Andes **46** E3
Andhra Pradesh □ **25** D6
Andorra ■ **9** A6
Andreanof Is. **38** C2
Ándria **12** D7
Andros I. **45** C9
Angara → **18** D11
Ånge **6** F11
Angel Falls **46** B3
Angerman → **6** F11
Angers **8** C3
Anglesey **7** E4
Angola ■ **33** G3
Angoulême **8** D4
Angoumois **8** D3
Anguilla ■ **44** J18
Anhui □ **21** C6
Anjou **8** C3
Ankara **15** G5
Ann, C. **43** D12
Ann Arbor **42** D6
Annaba **28** A6
Annapolis **42** F9
Annecy **8** D7
Annobón **27** G4
Anshun **20** D5
Antalya **15** G5
Antananarivo **33** H9
Antarctic Pen. **48** D4
Antibes **8** E7
Anticosti I. **43** A16
Antigua Barbuda ■ **44** K20
Antofagasta **47** E2
Antsiranana **33** G9
Antwerp **10** C3
Anyang **21** C6
Aomori **19** F12
Aparri **22** B4
Apeldoorn **10** B3
Apennines **12** B4
Apia **35** C16
Appalachian Mts. **42** G7
Appleton **42** C3
Aqmola **18** D9
Ar Ramadi **24** B3
Arabian Desert **29** C11
Arabian Gulf = Gulf, The **24** C4
Arabian Sea **24** D5
Aracaju **46** D6
Arad **11** E11
Arafura Sea **22** D5
Aragón □ **9** B5
Araguaia → **46** C5
Arak **24** B3
Arakan Yoma **25** C8
Aral **18** E8
Aral Sea **18** E8
Arcachon **8** D3
Arctic Ocean **48** B17
Arctic Red River **38** B6
Ardabil **24** B3
Ardennes **10** D3
Arendal **6** G9
Arequipa **46** D2
Argentan **8** B3
Argentina ■ **47** F3
Arima **44** S20
Arizona □ **40** D4
Arkansas □ **41** D8
Arkansas → **41** D8
Arkhangelsk **14** B7
Arles **8** E6
Arlington **42** F9
Arlon **10** D3
Armenia ■ **15** F7
Arnhem **10** C3
Arnhem Land **34** C5
Arnprior **42** C9
Arrah **23** G10
Arran **7** D4
Arras **8** A5
Artois **8** A5
Aru Is. **22** D5
Arunachal Pradesh □ **25** C8
Arusha **32** E7
Asab **31** B2
Asahigawa **19** F12
Asansol **23** H11
Asbestos **43** C12
Asbury Park **43** E10
Ascension I. **27** G2
Ashkhabad **18** F7
Ashland, Ky., U.S.A. **42** F6
Ashland, Ohio, U.S.A. **42** E6
Ashtabula **42** E7
Asifabad **23** K7
Asir □ **24** D3
Asmara **29** E12
Assam □ **23** F13
Assen **10** B4
Assisi **12** C5
Asti **12** B3
Astrakhan **15** E8
Asturias □ **9** A3
Asunción **47** E4
Aswân **29** D11
Atacama Desert **47** E3
Atbara **29** E11
Atbara → **29** E11
Athabasca → **38** C8
Athabasca, L. **38** C9
Athens, Greece **13** F10
Athens, U.S.A. **42** F6
Atikokan **42** A2
Atlanta **41** D10
Atlantic City **43** F10
Atlantic Ocean **2** E9
Atyraū **18** E7
Au Sable → **42** C6
Aube → **8** B5
Auburn, Ind., U.S.A. **42** E5
Auburn, N.Y., U.S.A. **42** D9
Aubusson **8** D5
Auch **8** E4
Auckland **35** H13
Aude → **8** E5
Augrabies Falls **31** B3
Augsburg **10** D6
Augusta, Ga., U.S.A. **41** D10
Augusta, Maine, U.S.A. **43** C13
Aunis **8** C3
Aurangabad, Bihar, India **23** G10
Aurangabad, Maharashtra, India **23** K5
Aurillac **8** D5
Aurora **42** E3
Austin **40** D7
Australia ■ **34** E5
Australian Alps **34** H8
Australian Capital Territory □ **34** H8
Austria ■ **10** E8
Autun **8** C6
Auvergne **8** D5
Auxerre **8** C5
Avallon **8** C5
Avellino **12** D6
Avignon **8** E6
Ávila **9** B3
Avranches **8** B3
Axiós → **13** D10
Ayers Rock **34** F5
Ayr **7** D4
Azamgarh **23** F9
Azerbaijan ■ **15** F8
Azores **2** C8
Azov, Sea of **15** E6
Azuero Pen. **45** F8

Babol **24** B4
Babuyan Chan. **22** B4
Bacău **11** E14
Bacolod **22** B4
Bad Axe **42** D6
Badajoz **9** C2
Badalona **9** B7
Baden-Württemberg □ **10** D5
Baffin I. **39** B12
Baghdad **24** B3
Baguio **22** B4
Bahamas ■ **45** C10
Baharampur **23** G12
Bahawalpur **23** E3
Bahía = Salvador **46** D6
Bahía □ **46** D5
Bahía Blanca **47** F3
Bahraich **23** F8
Bahrain ■ **24** C4
Baia Mare **11** E12
Baie-St-Paul **43** B12
Baikal, L. **18** D12
Baja California **44** B2
Bakersfield **40** C3
Bakhtaran **24** B3
Baku **15** F8
Balabac Str. **22** C3
Balaghat **23** J8
Balaton **11** E9
Balboa **44** H14
Baldwin **42** D5
Balearic Is. **9** C7
Baleshwar **23** J11
Bali **22** D3
Balikeşir **13** E12
Balikpapan **22** D3
Balkan Mts. **13** C10
Balkhash, L. **18** E9
Ballarat **34** H7
Balqash **18** E9
Balrampur **23** F9
Balsas → **44** D4
Baltic Sea **6** G11
Baltimore **42** F9
Bam **24** C4
Bamako **28** F3
Bamberg **10** D6
Bamenda **30** C4
Bancroft **42** C9
Banda **23** G8
Banda Aceh **22** C1
Banda Is. **22** D4
Banda Sea **22** D4
Bandar Abbas **24** C4
Bandar Khomeyni **24** B3
Bandar Seri Begawan **22** C3
Bandundu **32** E3
Bandung **22** D2
Bangalore **25** D6
Banggai Arch. **22** D4
Bangka **22** D2
Bangka Str. **22** D2
Bangkok **22** B2
Bangladesh ■ **23** H13
Bangor **43** C13
Bangui **32** D3
Bangweulu, L. **32** G6
Banja Luka **12** B7
Banjarmasin **22** D3
Banjul **28** F1
Banks I. **38** A7
Bankura **23** H11
Bannu **23** C3
Banská Bystrica **11** D10
Banyak Is. **22** C1
Baoding **21** C6
Baoji **20** C5
Baotou **21** B6
Bar Harbor **43** C13
Bar-le-Duc **8** B6
Baracaldo **9** A4
Baramula **23** B5
Baran **23** G6
Baranovichi **11** B14
Barbados ■ **44** P22
Barberton, S. Africa **31** B5
Barberton, U.S.A. **42** E7
Barcelona **9** B7
Barddhaman **23** H11
Bardstown **42** G5
Bareilly **23** E7
Barents Sea **48** B8
Barhi **23** G10
Bari **12** D7
Bari Doab **23** D4
Barisal **23** H13
Barito → **22** D3
Barkly Tableland **34** D6
Barkly West **31** B3
Barletta **12** D7
Barmer **23** G3
Barnaul **18** D10
Barques, Pt. Aux **42** C6
Barquísimeto **46** A3
Barrancabermeja **46** B2
Barranquilla **46** A2
Barre **43** C11
Barrie **42** C8
Barry's Bay **42** C9
Bashkortostan □ **14** D10
Basilan **22** C4
Baskatong, Rés. **43** B10
Basle **10** E4
Basque Provinces = País Vasco □ **9** A4
Basra **24** B3
Bass Str. **34** H8
Basse-Terre **44** M20
Bassein **25** D8
Basseterre **44** K19
Basti **23** F9
Bastia **8** E8
Bata **32** D1
Batangas **22** B4
Batavia **42** D8
Bath, U.K. **7** F5
Bath, Maine, U.S.A. **43** D13
Bath, N.Y., U.S.A. **42** D9
Bathurst, Australia **34** G8
Bathurst, Canada **43** B15
Batna **28** A6
Baton Rouge **41** D8
Battambang **22** B2
Batticaloa **25** E7
Battle Creek **42** D5
Batu Is. **22** D1
Batu Pahat **22** C2
Batumi **15** F7
Bavaria = Bayern □ **10** D6
Bawean **22** D3
Bay City **42** D6
Bayamo **45** C9
Bayan Har Shan **20** C4
Bayern □ **10** D6
Bayeux **8** B3
Bayonne **8** E3
Bayrūt **24** B2
Beacon **43** E11
Beagle, Canal **47** H3
Béarn **8** E3
Beauce, Plaine de la **8** B4
Beaufort Sea **48** B18
Beaufort West **31** C3
Beauharnois **43** C11
Beaumont **41** D8
Beaune **8** C6
Beauvais **8** B5
Beaver Falls **42** E7
Beaver I. **42** C5
Beawar **23** F5
Béchar **28** B4
Beckley **42** G7
Bedford, Ind., U.S.A. **42** F4
Bedford, Va., U.S.A. **42** G8
Bei'an **21** B7
Beijing **21** C6
Beira **33** H6
Békéscsaba **11** E11
Bela **23** F1
Belarus ■ **11** B14
Belau = Palau ■ **36** G5
Belaya Tserkov **11** D16
Belcher Is. **39** C12
Belém **46** C5
Belfast, S. Africa **31** B5
Belfast, U.K. **7** D4
Belfast, U.S.A. **43** C13
Belfort **8** C7
Belgaum **25** D6
Belgium ■ **10** C3
Belgorod **15** D6
Belgrade **13** B9
Beliton Is. **22** D2
Belize ■ **44** D7
Belize City **44** D7
Bellaire **42** E7
Bellary **25** D6
Belle-Ile **8** C2
Belle Isle, Str. of **39** C14
Bellefontaine **42** E6
Belleville **42** C9
Bellingshausen Sea **48** D3
Bellinzona **10** E5
Belmopan **44** D7
Belo Horizonte **46** D5

AFGHANISTAN	ALBANIA	ALGERIA	ANDORRA	ANGOLA	ANTIGUA & BARBUDA	ARGENTINA
BARBADOS	BELGIUM	BELIZE	BELARUS	BENIN	BHUTAN	BOLIVIA
BURUNDI	CAMBODIA	CAMEROON	CANADA	CAPE VERDE	CENTRAL AFRICAN REP	CHAD
CUBA	CYPRUS	CZECH REPUBLIC	DENMARK	DJIBOUTI	DOMINICA	DOMINICAN REPUBL
FAROE ISLANDS	FIJI	FINLAND	FRANCE	GABON	GAMBIA	GEORGIA
GUINEA-BISSAU	GUYANA	HAITI	HONDURAS	HONG KONG	HUNGARY	ICELAND
IVORY COAST	JAMAICA	JAPAN	JORDAN	KAZAKSTAN	KENYA	KIRIBATI
LESOTHO	LIBERIA	LIBYA	LIECHTENSTEIN	LITHUANIA	LUXEMBOURG	MACAU
MAURITANIA	MAURITIUS	MEXICO	MICRONESIA	MOLDOVA	MONACO	MONGOLIA
NICARAGUA	NIGER	NIGERIA	NORTHERN MARIANAS	NORWAY	OMAN	PAKISTAN
PUERTO RICO	QATAR	ROMANIA	RUSSIA	RWANDA	SAN MARINO	SÃO TOMÉ & PRÍNCI
SOLOMON ISLANDS	SOMALIA	SOUTH AFRICA	SPAIN	SRI LANKA	ST KITTS & NEVIS	ST LUCIA
TAIWAN	TAJIKISTAN	TANZANIA	THAILAND	TOGO	TONGA	TRINIDAD & TOBAG
UNITED KINGDOM	UNITED STATES	URUGUAY	UZBEKISTAN	VANUATU	VATICAN CITY	VENEZUELA